BOBOLOGY

THE REAL JESUS

Bob Evans

All proceeds are for the Liverpool Seafarers Centre, 20, Crosby Road South, Liverpool. L22 1RQ Registered with the Charity Commission. No. 1125539

Liverpool Seafarers Centre
A Lifeline for Seafarers

For my family

Previous books by Bob Evans

A Dog Collar in the Docks
Mersey Mariners
The Way to Liverpool
The Training Ships of Liverpool
HMS EAGLET
The INDEFATIGABLE
The Mersey Mission to Seafarers
A Lantern on the Stern
Volume One The Early Years
Volume Two The Later Years
Volume Three The Story Never Ends
Volume Four More Tales of the Sea
The Conway Heroes
Charlie the Mouse

First Published 2010 by Countyvise Limited,
14 Appin Road, Birkenhead, Wirral CH41 9HH.

British Library Cataloguing in Publication Data.
A catalogue record for this book is available from the British Library.

ISBN 978 1 906205 40 9

PREFACE

Bobology may seem rather an odd title for a book and must be explained. Most of my life has been involved with theology, which should be no surprise to anyone. There have been so many books, most rather long, some almost unintelligible, some a total joy. Inevitably, as you grow rather ancient as I have, you become very selective of all dogma … this is what the 'University of Life' does to you. Theology is written by other people and if it is to be of any value, the 'God-thoughts' have to become your thoughts. That is what this book is all about … my thoughts about Jesus.

So whatever your name is, make theology your thoughts … Stephenology, Janeology or Martinology. It takes courage to walk this path. William Drummond got it right in an age when questions were not allowed.

> 'He who will not reason is a bigot,
> He who cannot is a fool;
> He who dare not is a slave.'
>
> William Drummond (1585-1649)
> Academical Question.

At the age of eighty-six, I decided that it was time for some Bobology. I do not ask you to agree with any of my thoughts, but I hope that you will afford me tolerance and love and a little understanding. For the last fifty years, my life in the Port of Liverpool has been involved with the nations of the world and with the world religions. Seafarers are excellent listeners and talkers; they are totally tolerant of each other and they understand the need to live together in harmony in their small communities aboard ship. Bigotry has no place in a seafarer's life. Together we shared our religions and I discovered how we could live together, each man with his faith.

During my lifetime there have been dramatic developments in our studies of the life of Jesus. American theologians and in this country the Bishop of Durham, N.T. Wright, have helped to transform my understanding of Jesus. I was taught at university over sixty years ago that all theological conundrums had been resolved by the fourth century and was assured that armed with the Bible and Cranmer's Book of Common Prayer, my training was complete. There was to be nothing new; that was all that was apparently needed to become a parson. 'As it was in the beginning is now ever shall be' about summed up my mental state.

The 'Death of God' controversy in the 60s was the initial shock to my ecclesiastical compliance with the 'truth'. It was like starting all over again in my search for Jesus.

My faith had to be re-thought. I have discovered that it is possible to be both liberal and orthodox in my thinking … I am not a slave to dogma. I have found a Christ who sets me free. It has been an exciting journey.

Writing this book has been a labour of love and has been

a good discipline for my mind and my soul. I have discussed its contents with many folk, but especially with my good friend Colin Lee ... in fact, every word in the writing of every paragraph has been shared with him. My thanks go to Bill Wood, the Reverend John Williams, Peter and Barbara Leach, Nevil James, and to the family ... Brigita, Stephen, Jane, John, Heather and Martin. The Majestas on page 126 was drawn by Martin. They have all made valuable contributions and often spared little mercy in their comments. Jean and John Emmerson, the publishers, have as ever been helpful and patient. However, the opinions, blemishes, mistakes and misjudgements can only be attributed to me. Incidentally, the Bible text I've used is from the New English Bible - now out of print, but much admired by me.

All that I ask of the reader is patience, tolerance, love and understanding.

Bob Evans
Liverpool
2010

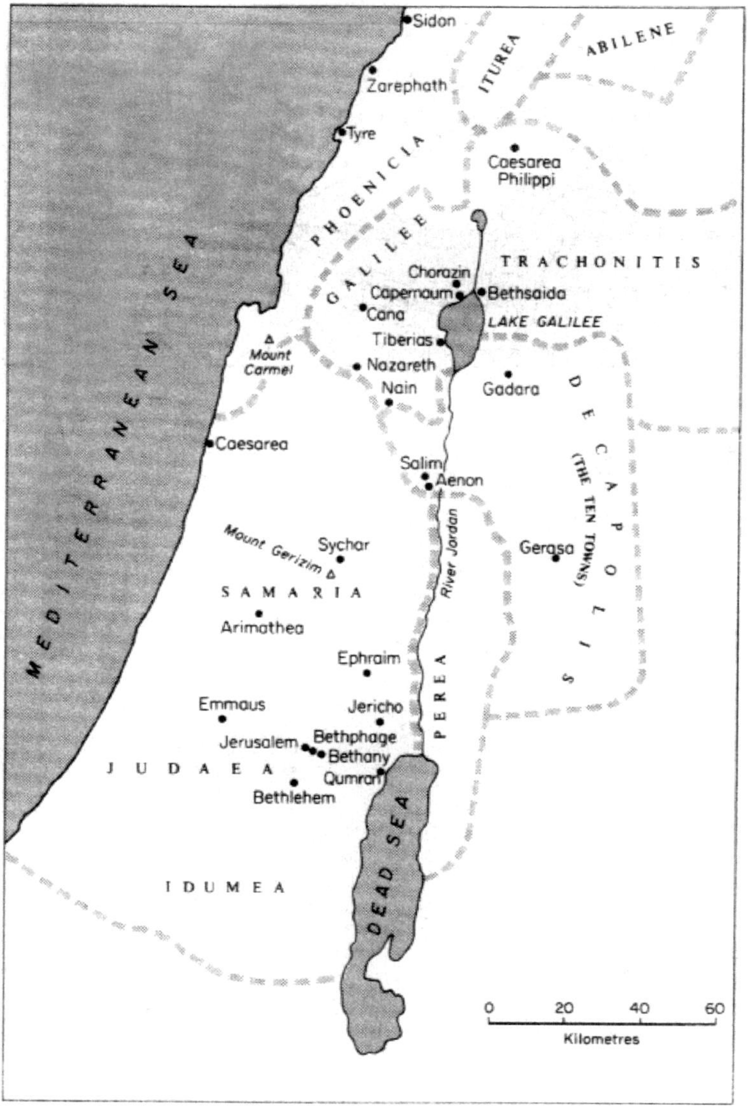
Sidon
ABILENE
ITUREA
Zarephath
Tyre
Caesarea Philippi
PHOENICIA
GALILEE
TRACHONITIS
MEDITERRANEAN SEA
Chorazin
Capernaum
Bethsaida
Cana
LAKE GALILEE
Tiberias
Mount Carmel
Nazareth
Nain
Gadara
DECAPOLIS
(THE TEN TOWNS)
Caesarea
Salim
Aenon
Mount Gerizim
Sychar
River Jordan
Gerasa
SAMARIA
Arimathea
Ephraim
PEREA
Emmaus
Jericho
Jerusalem
Bethphage
Bethany
JUDAEA
Qumran
Bethlehem
DEAD SEA
IDUMEA
0
20
40
60
Kilometres

CONTENTS

The Liverpool Cathedral Cross

Chapter One

WHAT CAN I BELIEVE?

'He who will not reason is a bigot,
He who cannot is a fool;
He who dare not is a slave.'
William Drummond (1585-1649)
Academical Question.

Working for some three decades in the docks of Liverpool, meeting men on the ships from all the nations of the world, enjoying close contact with all the world religions … all of this surely colours your life and your thinking.

Was it aboard the JALAJOTI that I found myself in a cabin surrounded by seafarers and, to my surprise, the subject under discussion was 'God'? There was no anger or bigotry; we were all interested in each others journey into the unknown. We all had our own ideas as we all came from different backgrounds. We spoke and we listened. Eventually one man summed it all up.

"You Gupta, you Ali, you Mohammed, you Josh, you Jal, you Bhindi, you Gobi, you Bob … all different, but there can only be one God!"

That about got it right for me and I had learnt again the main maxim for a Mission to Seamen Padre … 'It's better to listen and learn than pontificate.'

I was born in 1924 in South Wales and lived in a small village called Llanharan in the Vale of Glamorgan. It was a safe and happy place for a child. There were no cinemas, television, discos, libraries, banks, swimming pool, social services … I suppose that by modern criteria it would be classified as a deprived area. It didn't feel like it. We never locked the doors of our homes. We children wandered the hills around us and swam in the streams. It was a carefree life. There was little, if any, crime. I knew about the crime statistics in our village … my father was the local police sergeant, with two constables and a cell in which they stored the filing system! The population was under two thousand and we boasted three pubs, two chippies, six chapels and a church. My family was regarded as 'posh' and naturally we went to the church … in those days we called it the 'Church of England in Wales' … later, 'The Church of Wales'. There were three car owners in the village … the vicar, the doctor and my dad … and we children played in the middle of the roads. Most of us spoke Welsh at home, but once we went to school we had to learn 'the English' in order to be educated!

I really left the village at the age of eleven when I went to Grammar School in Bridgend, seven miles away, and discovered a library for the first time in my life … it was gold.

Religion played an important part in my upbringing. Church three times on Sunday, choir boy at seven, there were concerts and plays, debating societies and, above all, we had tonic-sol-fa which meant that we could all sing our choral parts with ease … soprano, alto, tenor and bass. We could harmonise a railway time-table!

The word 'religion' is a Latin word ... religio ... 'what binds you together'. It meant that the village was a family and, when someone died, the whole village mourned. In a real sense our church-going did bind us together as a community.

Then there was rugby, tennis, cricket, bowls, summer fetes, push-football, slow bicycle races, athletics, eventually a cinema and the wireless. I was fourteen when electric light came to the village and I no longer studied by oil lamp and candle light.

Next came University for a year, then flying in the Royal Air Force as a pilot mainly in Rhodesia, another four years back at university and then I wrapped a dog-collar around my neck in July 1950 at the age of twenty-six.

I started my ministry in a mining village in Aberdare, then I worked in the shadow of Tiger Bay and the Dowlais steel works in Cardiff. Next came the luxury of Llandaff Cathedral, before I arrived in Liverpool. It was rather a long time ago that Liverpool became my real home. I was the Chaplain Superintendent of the Mersey Mission to Seafarers

Liverpool was a shock. Ships, seafarers and a truly cosmopolitan city! Liverpool was a conurbation of some three million people and the port was the gateway into the world.

You never forget the first time that you walk cold aboard a ship. You are a stranger and you have to win the confidence of those on board. This was a challenge and I had to get it right first time, or fail and scuttle back to the safety of parish life where I had learned my trade. In a parish you tend to meet your own folk and have little time to worry about the rest of the population. Parish life was no sinecure and I had enjoyed it. I had worked hard with some success and contentment, but it was not enough. My new parish in Liverpool embraced people from all over the world, all colours, all faiths and many with no faith at all. Happily, I quickly realised that my main purpose was to establish friendships. That was the starting block.

An old friend once told me how to sell Wrens boot polish. He was good at it.

> You have to believe that you have the best product in the world.
>
> You have to meet your customer where they are and not where you think they are.
>
> You have to be acceptable to them as a person.

The main objective was to establish a friendship. If, after the initial ship visit, the next time when you board that ship, you meet someone who regards you as a friend … you have arrived. A man will never use you as a Padre unless he can trust you. You have established a friendship. It's all rather basic but it works.

So there I was … in the middle of the world religions and on a steep learning curve. The simplest thing would have been to close my mind and think as an Anglican priest and as a Christian. That would have been too easy and I would have been very lonely … and I would have been of no value to anyone. Very quickly I realised that I was there to learn and share, and not to convert or instruct or condemn. This was a new experience.

Then I discovered the secret of all religions. All the world religions are based upon the dynamic power of love and if they are not, they are worthless. Judge every thing and every person by the word 'love'. That was very helpful to me as a Christian because it had long dawned upon me that 'God is love' is a basic concept of my faith. And that had little to do with Archbishops, Diocesan Synods and the Thirty-nine Articles of Religion to which my church at that time demanded my assent!

I knew exactly where I was going. Jesus had faced the same challenge as me. They tried to trap him, but he had the answer. This religion stuff is simple. There are just two things to remember and Jesus knew it! 'Love God and love your neighbour'. How more basic can you get than that? It solves all the problems of mankind and is common to all religions. It would end all the strife in the world, sort out our domestic problems and bring peace to mankind. We would even share our food and no-one would die of starvation. 'Love God and love your neighbour' does not need politics or atom bombs or the United Nations Assembly to enforce it. Anger, jealousy, greed, murder, rape and genocide would be no more.

For thirty years in the docks of Liverpool, that was all the ammunition that I needed. I could talk to anyone with the security of 'having the best product in the world'. And it was this man, Jesus, who had shown me the way, taught me the basic truth and had given me a light on my path through life.

At last I could relax and feel at home with mankind. There was no need to teach or pontificate, my task was simply to enjoy the company of seafarers and share our journey to discover the secret of living. For the last sixty years of my life that is exactly what I have done. If you have no love … you are nothing.

In this little book I want to share the fun of that journey across the decades. It really has been fun. I have learned to laugh and smile and be at home with the peoples of the world. At the same time I have also shared the pain and anguish of mankind.

The main task in my thinking has been to abandon as useless most of the ecclesiastical baggage which we Christians seem to have accumulated over two thousand years. You may not agree and you may even be offended by my discoveries, but all that I ask is that you do not write me off as a heretic or a Philistine or a non-believer or whatever comes to your mind … all that I ask is that you surround me with your love, because like the rest of mankind that is all that we need.

Above all, please stay with me as I attempt to discover what Jesus would have me do with my life.

What am I to believe?

'Love God and love your neighbour'.

Chapter Two

THE WORLD OF JESUS

We all start at the beginning, but it is not easy to decide when that actually is. I cannot define the beginning of my 'call' to be a Christian. There was never a time when I wanted to become anything except a parson.

It was a form of innocence and it did create the odd problem as I grew up in my small Welsh village in the Vale of Glamorgan. There was one confrontation that remains etched into my memory. The gentleman was called Johnny Pinkott.

Johnny had religion in a big way, but was suspect because he was neither Church nor Chapel. He was a free thinking evangelical with the gall to mention God on other days apart from Sunday and this he did in the street with legs apart, arms up in the air and in a loud voice. All denominations frowned upon him, as he caused discomfort with all his chat about God. This was used as proof that Johnny was not quite with us. It was the simplest explanation of his apparent nodding acquaintance with the Almighty.

One day, I met Johnny Pinkott head-on in the Square, outside Bert Beard's the Blacksmith. There was no escape. He stood bandy legged, armed with a walking stick, baggy black trousers, no tie and a battered hat.

"I believe you are going into the Church, boy."

This was a powerful opening broadside for a fifteen year old with little to say and even that with a stammer. My silence was not noticed, as he went in for the killer punch.

"Has God spoken to you?"

My dumbness was complete, which was just as well, as Johnny was not indulging in a discussion.

"God spoke to me in Porthcawl."

He waved his arm in the vague direction of that seaside resort.

"I was standing on the promenade, watching the sea, and placed my hands on the railings. They were vibrating with power and that was when God spoke to me."

Suddenly, he seemed to expect me to speak.

I had nothing to say. Johnny turned and left me with no further explanation, heading for Reg Smith the Butcher, his stick acting like a rudder as his legs shot out sideways with minds of their own. I worried. I, too, had stood on the promenade at Porthcawl, as the sea crashed magnificently over the top and all that I had done was lick ice-cream. God must have been very selective to pick on Johnny.

Jesus grew up in a small village not much different from Llanharan and faced the same world as I did all those years ago. He, like all of us, was shaped by the political and religious background of his day.

Politically the entire western world was dominated by the Roman Empire … Augustus (31 BC-AD 14) and Tiberius (AD 14-37). To understand Jesus we must uncover the prime influences on his life. They were to test and create his main message for mankind.

The political centre was Judea with the headquarters at Caesarea Maritime. The religious centre was Jerusalem … controlled by the High Priest, who was advised by the council, the Sanhedrin. The High Priest was held in high regard by the Roman authority and by the majority of the Jews.

The Pharisees (from the Hebrew word 'separated) were the spiritual leaders and they guided and controlled the synagogues … these were 'churches' scattered throughout the community. The Pharisees had fostered the oral tradition of learning the scriptures and dominated Jewish life and thought. They were virtually to disappear after the Jewish revolt against the Romans which started in AD 66.

The Sadducees were a conservative Jewish group, centred round the High Priest and they were much involved with the worship in the Temple at Jerusalem.

The Temple was the national shrine of Judaism and had been built in the tenth century BC, reconstructed by Zerubbabal later in the same century, and it was finally destroyed by the Roman army in AD 70 during the suppression of the Jewish revolt. The end of the Temple marked the end of the Sadducees.

The Scribes were 'the vicars' well versed in Judaism, preserving and expounding the Law and the faith, and mainly supported the Pharisees. Later such teachers were described as rabbis, and were the leaders in the synagogues.

Judaism was based on the law (the Torah the first five books of the Old Testament, which were called the Pentateuch) and on the prophets. Moses was regarded as the greatest prophet of them all. In the Old Testament we have fifteen individual prophets, dating from the eighth to the fifth century, after which there were no more.

In contrast, the Roman Empire was based on Emperor-worship and polytheism ... the worship of many gods.

Herod died in 4 BC having controlled Palestine for some thirty years. At his death his sons took over the kingdoms. Herod Antipas was to take over Jerusalem and the fertile area of Galilee. Rome was not very successful in ruling that region and it led to the Jewish revolts in AD 66-73 and 132-5. The revolts were important because they were to colour the New Testament writings, which fell within those dates.

Jesus lived and worked mainly in Galilee. The Galileans were Jews, but were regarded as aliens by the folk in Judea and in Jerusalem. We know little about his life until he was aged thirty. We believe that his father, Joseph, died when Jesus was a youth and presumably he had taught Jesus his trade as a carpenter. Jesus had domestic responsibilities. There was the family to care for ... his brothers and sisters.

His cousin, John, had broken away from his family and was living as an itinerant preacher. His name was becoming known and he was attracting a band of followers. He would have been the talk of the village gossips and his message about the coming of a kingdom would have grown in the telling. John the Baptist was a maverick, an odd-ball, a person to watch.

The Jews had had enough of the Roman domination and were obsessed with the possibility of a kingdom to release them from the power of Rome. They prayed that the revolution was imminent and led by the Messiah, their hoped-for King restoring their nation to what they imagined were former glories. The word 'kingdom' was their dream.

Jesus was to make the idea of a Kingdom his main theme. At the start of his ministry he returned to Nazareth, where he had been brought up, and went to the synagogue on the Sabbath day as he regularly did. He stood up to read the lesson and was handed the scroll of the prophet Isaiah. He opened the scroll and found the passage which says,

'The spirit of the Lord is upon me because he has anointed me;
He has sent me to announce good news to the poor,
To proclaim release for prisoners and recovery of sight for the blind;
To let the broken victims go free,
To proclaim the year of the Lord's favour.'

He rolled up the scroll, gave it back to the attendant, and sat down; and all eyes in the synagogue were fixed on him.

He began to speak: 'Today', he said, 'in your very hearing this text has come true.' There was a general stir of admiration; they were surprised that words of such grace should fall from his lips. 'Is not this Joseph's son?' they asked. Luke 4. 16-22

This amazed his listeners … it was a startling message about the Kingdom. The word 'kingdom' appears thirty-seven times in Matthew, who tends to use the phrase Kingdom of Heaven, and thirty-two times in Luke. It was the basis of our Lord's teaching. It was a concept well documented in the Old Testament and the Jews believed that all history was foretold in their scriptures. The Jews believed that everything in life was planned by God and that especially included their history ... all happenings were foretold in the holy books. Those early Christians felt the same and naturally it was to colour their writings. Often the story of Jesus was to be changed in order to conform to scripture ... his life had to conform to scripture!

The new concept announced by Jesus was the imminence of the Kingdom.

'From that day Jesus began to proclaim the message: "Repent for the kingdom of heaven is upon you."'

Matthew 4. 17

'The time has come; the kingdom of God is upon you; repent, and believe the Gospel.'

Mark 1. 15

Jesus also talked about the end of the world and suggested that it was not very far off. It became obvious in time that in this prediction, Jesus was mistaken ... the fact that he was in error was to prove great concern for the early Christians. How could Jesus be wrong? Jesus was presumed to be infallible. Also it seemed to contradict his statement that 'the end' was already here ... that was his startling twist in John the Baptist's teaching. "The Kingdom of God is among you." That phrase has caused much misunderstanding as the Greek word can be translated as either 'among' or 'within'. Whilst we tend to accept the spiritual word 'within', Jesus probably meant no more than ... the Kingdom is here now. In reality, that does not rule out the thought that there will be a final 'end'. Later Christians were to suggest that the final end would be the return of Christ, the Second Coming and Final Judgement. But Jesus seemed more concerned in the preparation of his own disciples for the immediate coming of the Kingdom … be alert and do not be caught sleeping. That was the essence of his moral teaching. Jesus was interested in the present moment.

'Set your mind upon his kingdom, and all the rest will come to you as well.'

Luke 12. 31.

Jesus had a deep sense of urgency.

'I tell you, whoever does not accept the kingdom of God like a child will never enter it.'

Mark 10. 15.

Children are receptive and that quality is essential if we are to accept the Kingdom of God.

We shall also discover that Jesus gave us two very simple rules for the Kingdom … love God and love your neighbour. These were not original as they emerge from the Old Testament, but he makes them paramount for our entry into the Kingdom. However, it was asking much for the Jews to love the occupants of their country!

We are called to be Kingdom people and it is with that thought in my mind that I now move on to examine the life of Jesus.

Chapter Three

DID CHRIST EXIST?

At no time for me had there been any flashing lights, no crash of thunder, not even a small still voice. I just knew that I wanted to be a parson and had made that quite clear to the family at an early age. The local incumbents in turn, Vicar Jones and Vicar Corney, had led me through the early years as a choir boy and then an altar server.

Vicar Corney had briefed me at the age of fifteen, before I travelled to Llandaff to meet the forbidding Bishop John Morgan. The Bishop, I assumed, wanted to question my vocation. I had never talked to a Bishop and was looking forward to a new experience. My Vicar stressed one point to remember during my interview.

"Don't mention music because the Bishop is an expert."

All advice is good when you are going into the unknown, armed with the ignorance and the assurance of youth. That interview with the good Bishop remains in the archives of my mind.

The Bishop's Palace at Llandaff was large and I felt very small as I entered the open door, clutching my Bridgend Grammar School cap for protection. There was no need to be nervous. The Bishop was great.

A large dog had sniffed me as I went into the Palace and, then, in the hall, the Bishop threw a ball down the passage.

Off the hound went, putting on his brakes half way along to end up in a heap at the far wall. I was promptly dispatched to the opposite end and eventually finished with the ball in my hand and the dog on top with its legs pinning me against the wall. Then we sat on the floor, in front of the study fire, to enjoy tea and cream cakes. I had forgotten that it was called 'an interview'. The Bishop chatted away, popping in the occasional question. One stopped me in my tracks.

"Do you knit?"

My astonishment must have shown. He went on to explain that men were often the best designers, the top chefs and the finest painters. The word 'chauvinism' was not in common use in those days, but I suspect that the Bishop would have said that he was only stating the obvious. I nodded as wisely as I could.

"Do you like music?"

There it was, the trap question, and I fell for it, lulled by cakes and dogs and Episcopal guile.

"Yes, I love music."

"What do you make of Bela Bartok?"

For all that I knew it was a skin disease. I had never heard of the name!

"I love the psalms."

The Bishop beamed and went across to his grand piano. We sang. I still had the remnants of a treble voice and together we delighted in the 23rd and the 150th psalms. Here was a man who understood that in Llanharan the only available music was to be found in the Church choir, and that was what we discussed.

We talked of David John Kinsey, our choir master, who made the boys feel his tummy as he breathed in deeply and, in turn, showed us how to fill our lungs. We chatted about Miss Jones, who treadled her way on the swaying harmonium, holding on to the bottom note long after we had run out of puff. Bishop John Morgan accepted me as an ordinand and some ten years later he was to ordain me.

I wonder whether Jesus had much the same experiences as he grew into manhood. We have hardly any clues to guide us, but it is time to look hard at him. If he is the gateway to God, he is vital to our journey.

My quiet reflections over the decades have convinced me that we have attributed words and deeds and expectations to Christ that, I suspect, would surprise him. It is precisely what time does to memories ... colour, expand and distort, yet hopefully the central core will remain. There is a punch-line to every story and that gives the story life, otherwise it would not be remembered or recorded. Jesus lived for a mere thirty years or so and we only have partial records for the few final years, probably no more than four. And it was all rather a long time ago.

I have to find this Jesus as best I can with the evidence that has remained for me to study. There are the Bible tales, barely remembered, often contradictory, not much more than glimpses, yet invaluable.

Of course there are problems. I can barely remember a shopping list dictated to me half an hour before I arrive in the store, so I must take into account that the Gospel accounts were written at least forty years after the event. It would seem that we are safer to regard them as reflections of devout minds thinking about Jesus and certainly not as verbatim accounts. That would start to explain the inconsistencies and contradictions.

Probing the life of Jesus is not going to be easy. We Christians have been trained to absorb Sunday by Sunday the drama of his life and the doctrines that have evolved from them. The Bible stories were partially assembled for that very purpose … they cannot be fully trustworthy as most eyewitnesses were long dead when they were written.

The Bible inevitably contains inconsistencies. A good example is found in the Resurrection story. Mark states that a young man was present when the women came to the tomb; Matthew says it was an angel; Luke says it was two men; John says two angels. This evidence seems somewhat confused. Each report is different, yet there will be a kernel of truth.

Then there are rather obvious contradictions … or are they just isolated recollections which inevitably can lead to confusion? The passage about the sheep and the goats in Matthew states that Jesus will turn to those on his left-hand … the goats … and say, "The curse is upon you; go from my sight to the eternal fire that is ready for the devil and his angels. For when I was hungry you gave me nothing to eat." Matthew 25. 41-42. Not much evidence of love there! But Luke says that when Jesus was not just hungry, but was being put to death, He said, "Father, forgive them for they know not what they do". Luke 23. 34. There is a contradiction between these two statements! I suspect that we might conclude that the former is just a story and the latter hard and cruel fact. So both memories are to be accepted.

A brief snap-shot of how the Gospels came into being is essential to our search for the real Jesus. The first three Gospels are interdependent ... we call them the Synoptic Gospels because they reflect the same view of Jesus. The fourth stands almost in isolation.

Matthew and Luke certainly use almost the whole of Mark as a prime source. Matthew (M) had material peculiar to his Gospel as also did Luke (L). We are convinced that there is an unknown source (Q). This leaves us with six linked sources of information about Jesus ... Mark, Q, Matthew, M (special Matthean material), Luke and L (special Lucan material). Also remember that there is the seventh source, the Gospel of John.

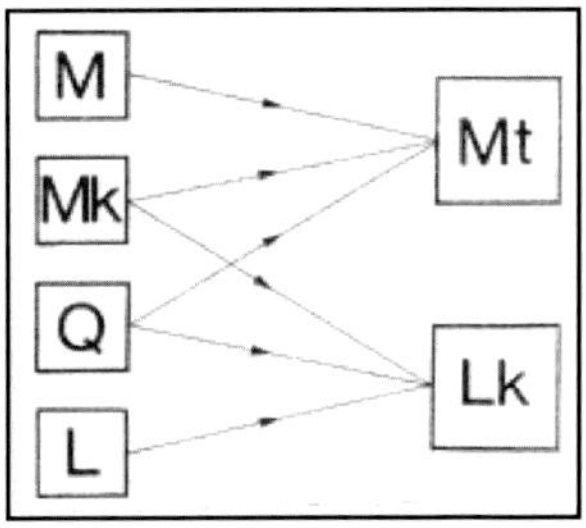

Q is postulated as a document, consisting mainly of sayings of Jesus, conventionally called Q (from the German *Quelle,* 'source'.) Q was probably written in the late fifties and modern scholars have 'put it together' from the material found in Matthew and Luke, but not in Mark. Mark knew nothing about the Q document. There are about two hundred verses, obviously copied from a written work and found in Matthew and Luke. They are a collection of teaching materials attributed to Jesus with hardly any narrative.

It is often forgotten that the earliest author in the New Testament was Paul. His letters were all written before the

Gospels, maybe twenty years before Mark, but as Paul says very little about Jesus, he is not a major source in the search for the historical Jesus.

Did Jesus actually exist or is he fabrication of human minds? What if the whole business about the origins of Christianity is a lie! The publication of *Holy Blood, Holy Grail,* the machinations of *The Da Vinci Code*, the postulation of a marriage between Jesus and Mary Magdelene, have all created a world-wide controversy. 'Mr. and Mrs. Jesus Christ' made rather a good sound-bite in the news. Jesus was back in the newspapers! Many people who had dismissed the Gospels as mumbo jumbo were aroused to ask questions about Jesus and Christianity and all that business recorded some two thousand years ago. Many thought that, at last, they could put these myths back into the time where they came from and forget them. It had nothing to do with them today.

The Jesus we think of today is barely visible in the Bible. Two thousand years of baggage has created a choice between the Christ of 'Gentle Jesus, meek and mild' and the misguided anarchist best forgotten about. Which was he? We are going to find that it is a long journey from a Galilean Jew of the first century to the concept of a risen Christ who is one with God.

There are two views of Jesus. There is the Jesus of history found in the Gospels and there is the Jesus of faith, who is also in the Gospels. These views are called the 'pre-Easter Jesus' and the 'post-Easter Jesus'. The first Jesus is 'dead and gone'; the second is alive and living in our experience. We must try to separate the pre-Easter Jesus from the post-Easter Jesus … the real historical Jesus from the Jesus created by faith. It is almost impossible to do this, but that is the task.

There are records apart from the New Testament. Tertullian (c. AD 160–225) states in his *Apologeticus* … 'All these things Pilate did to Christ … he sent word of Him to the reigning Caesar, who was at that time Tiberius.'

Pliny (AD 61-114) refers to Christians in his writing and states that they 'sang hymns to Christus as if he were a god.'

Tacitus (AD 55-120) was a Roman senator and met many Christians in his courtroom. He comments on the burning of Rome during the reign of Nero. 'Nero fabricated scapegoats … and punished with every refinement the notoriously depraved Christians (as they were popularly called). Their originator, Christ, had been executed in Tiberius's reign by the governor of Judaea, Pontius Pilate.'

Suetonius (AD 75-150) and Josephus (AD 37-100) both make firm reference to the historical existence of Jesus. Listen to what Josephus wrote. 'About that time lived Jesus, a wise man, if man he may be called, for he did wonderful works … a teacher of those who joyfully received the truth. He won to Himself many Jews and many Greeks. He was the Christ, and though Pilatus condemned him to death, He was our Messiah and appeared on the third day.'

There are also a number of Christian Gospels apart from the ones that we have nominated in the New Testament. The Gospel of Thomas is of special note. At the end of the nineteenth century many fragments of papyrus were found in a trash heap in Egypt. In the 1950s it was noticed that the writings were more important than the scholars had realised. The Gospel of Thomas really is an early Christian document and contains one hundred and fourteen sayings of Jesus.

Here is just one example. The Gospel of Thomas. 63.1-3

'Jesus said, "There was this rich person who had a great deal of money." He said "I shall invest my money so that I may sow, reap, plant, and fill my storerooms with produce, that I may lack nothing." These were the things he was thinking in his heart, but that night he died. Anyone here with two ears had better listen!'

Compare that version with Luke 12. 16-21. 'And he told them this parable: There was a rich man whose land yielded heavy crops. He debated with himself: "What am I to do? I have not the space to store my produce. This is what I will do," said he. "I will pull down my storehouses and build them bigger. I will collect in them all my corn and other goods, and then say to myself, 'Man, you have plenty of good things laid by, enough for many years: take life easy, eat, drink, and enjoy yourself.' But God said to him, "You fool, this very night you must surrender your life; you have made your money … who will get it now?" That is how it is with the man who amasses wealth for himself and remains a pauper in the sight of God.'

Thomas's version has simplicity with none of the moralising of Luke. His ending is abrupt and forceful; Luke makes far too much of the end and is almost sermonising. This suggests that Thomas is a pure oral saying, but Luke has done some editing. This suggests that Thomas is the earlier and more acceptable version.

In fact, the Gospel of Thomas provides us with eleven parables that are also found in the first three Gospels. We cannot ignore them.

We also have the Gospel of Peter and the Secret Gospel of Mark. There are many letters and documents. Perhaps there is no need to labour the point any longer. I accept that Jesus was not a figment of anyone's imagination. Jesus existed.

The quest for the historical Jesus has dominated us since the eighteenth century and we are still looking … it is proving to be an exciting search.

The four Gospels, as we have them, are the most important sources of information about the life of Jesus. However, there is a remarkable interest in the modern media concerning the Dead Sea Scrolls. They make good television programmes. We accept that they are possibly from the time of Jesus and as such are of value. They are manuscripts which were found in caves adjoining the Dead Sea and they illustrate the religious views of the community at Qumran. The community was an exclusive and semi-monastic sect, dating from BC 140 to 68 AD. Since 1947 many more such scrolls have been found and they help to fill in the social and political age in which Jesus lived. This community was called the Essenes and it is probable that John the Baptist was much influenced by them and thus, in turn, they did influence Jesus. We have tended to underplay the value of John the Baptist, but I regard him as a major force in formulating the message of Jesus. The concept of the Kingdom of God has firm roots in Qumran.

We cannot emphasise enough the fact that Jesus lived

in a time of great social change and tension. The Romans had taken charge some sixty years before the birth of Jesus. There were numerous revolts against the occupying force and some forty years after his death Jerusalem and the Temple were destroyed. This literally destroyed the world that Jesus had lived in and was a watershed in Jewish history. This surely led the early followers to grasp the message of Jesus as the way ahead … maybe all that they had left was a kingdom in heaven! Any concept of a kingdom on earth had been removed. Our four Gospels were written against a background of failure, political turmoil and anti-Jewish backlash. The Jewish world had been shattered.

Jesus probably wrote nothing and all our evidence rests on an oral tradition. It must be said that we have not a single word of Jesus nor a single story of Jesus that has not been processed through a believing congregation.

Jesus probably spoke in Galilean Aramaic, yet the Gospels are written in Greek. Translating from one language to another is notoriously problematic. Aramaic words often have a double meaning and the Greek translation might be in error. Take the parable of the servants to whom money was given. Matthew tells of three servants, each receiving five, two and one talent. In Luke we have ten servants, each receiving the same amount, but far less money than the Matthew account. So Luke has increased the servants and Matthew the amount of money. I accept that such contradictions do not alter the purpose of the parable. But they complicate the search for the historical, pre-Easter Jesus.

Whilst we really have no spoken words of Jesus, which are not 'second hand', there may be one exception and it is very important to our understanding of Jesus. The use by him of the Aramaic word 'abba' can only be pure Jesus-talk. He addressed God as 'abba'. The word 'abba' is the speech of children … Daddy! This is a Jesus word. In the time of Jesus children would use 'abba' to address their fathers with love. Jesus felt a love-relationship with God and 'abba' expressed just that. This was the love affair of Jesus.

My approach to the Gospels is rather basic after years of studying and attempting to understand the various theological postures that come and go … and come back again. How do we remember? We tend to recall events in our life which involved some form of trauma. A happy event today will remind me of a happy event fifty years ago. That is enough for me to think that I can remember all that happened around that memory. You can even recall conversations, smells, colour, but rarely dates! However, there is always a punch line that triggers that memory. Something happened … what was it? That is a fair question. There is always a punch line.

My basic approach is to look for the punch line in the Gospel stories and this possibly might help to uncover what really happened. There must be a truth behind each memory. I may never find the Jesus I am searching for, but that he is there is not in doubt.

Chapter Four

HOW DID IT REALLY START?

I like to ask friends to recall their first memory of childhood. The answers are fascinating and inevitably make for good conversation. My earliest recollection at about four years of age is revealing. Jim Davies, my play-pal from next door, was showing me his new toy … a tin fire-engine which had a lever to make it go forwards and backwards. I was obviously green with envy and the trauma of that triggered the memory.

But I was not prepared for this story of my life. My elder brother, Frank, was lost in March 1940 when his submarine, THISTLE, was sunk in the Baltic, torpedoed by a U-Boat. All hands died. Frank had joined the Royal Navy in 1936 and lived in married quarters in Plymouth. His family received six weeks notice to quit and a pension of twenty-five shillings … we will remember them! His wife, Zena, had two children both under the age of three and for a while we all lived together in Llanharan. Our bungalow was full. Zena, who was like a sister to me, died, aged ninety-six, last week and I remembered a letter that she had written to me on the 25th February, 1993. I copy it verbatim.

'Frank and I were staying at your bungalow in Llanharan. It must have been 1939 because Kay and Diane were babies. Late one evening we were talking to your parents

and we were remembering omens and odd experiences that we had all had. Dad with additions from Nana told us the following story, which they both swore was true and frightening.

Pat was a small baby when they received a message, via the police, that Henrietta had given birth to a baby boy and they were both dead.

As you can guess they were both devastated and were hurrying to visit Cilfynydd straight away.

Pat's cot was just behind the one armchair in front of the couch. It was a low, wooden cot on rockers, but Pat was in a bed.

Suddenly, they both saw your mother enter the room from the hall and, standing touching the cot, she looked straight at them ... then disappeared.

They rushed up to Cilfynydd to your home. Your father, grandmother and several neighbours were there, all very distressed and said no-one was to go upstairs to see mother and child as they were already in a coffin. As they had died of TB, no-one was to see them.

After a while they returned home and proceeded to get ready for bed. Dad was coming out of the bathroom, when he saw your mother again. Nana seeing his face quickly turned around and there was your mother again touching the cot.

So they drove back the twelve miles to Cilfynydd, where they were not welcomed, but Nana ran upstairs to the bedroom to find you in the coffin with your dead mother, very much alive.

Nana was hysterical and could not believe her eyes. She carried the baby downstairs, dressed him, and all the while

Grandma was saying "No! No! It's better to let him die. He will have TB too. And how can the child's father raise him and his sister Eunice on his own?"

So Nana said she would adopt him and bring him up with Pat and Frank. That was agreed as that was the only solution for your father.

At last they arrived home back in Llanharan with you all wrapped up and you were put into Pat's cot.

They didn't see your mother ever again, but they always knew that she wasn't very far away for those first few weeks.'

So it was that my aunt and uncle became my real mother and father.

I have discussed this letter many times with Zena and she has always insisted that her recollection of the story is accurate. This I have accepted and merely record it as it was written. During my lifetime I was never told anything of these events and as all my past family are no longer alive, I felt that it is opportune now to share the letter with you.

I wonder whether Jesus was ever told about the strange events surrounding his birth … I suspect the answer is no. Jesus never talked about his childhood and the remarkable accounts of his birth. One person asked me a good question recently "I wonder what happened to the gold and frankincense and myrrh?"

Father Christmas with all his tinsel and commercial mayhem has rather obscured the Gospel story. Some may think that the razzmatazz makes life easier for Christians. At least it is a popular happening. Everyone enjoys Christmas! I once heard someone say "The trouble with Christmas is that they keep bringing religion into it!" But there are, without doubt, problems.

The birth narratives in Matthew and in Luke differ from one another and are overgrown by legends and by Jewish and Christian conceptions of what should have happened. The story just grew and grew.

Without Matthew 1–2 and Luke 1–2 we would know nothing about the Christmas story. John has no need of it and neither does Paul nor Mark.

Christians have problems with Christmas. You must believe in Christmas if you are a Christian! If you don't, you are not. Others will insist that the divinity of Christ demands the Virgin Birth and others will suggest that that denies the humanity of Christ … he is not like us! Therefore, we cannot walk in his footsteps. Perhaps, we should just suspend our judgement because the birth stories might have little, if any, bearing upon the teaching of Jesus or upon his death. In other words, if Mark, John and Paul show no interest in the Christmas story, why should we?

Let us look at Christmas.

There is an enormous gap between what we proclaim in our Churches at Christmastide in the name of institutionalised Christianity and the record which we find in the Gospels. There are no camels for the wise men, no stable or animals. Check Matthew and Luke. The stories grew in the telling and, maybe as long as we accept them for what they are, there is little harm done.

The statement that 'he was born of the 'Virgin Mary' is questionable! Is the miraculous birth of Jesus a fact? Or is it a fable that has won acceptance in the passing of time? Was it based on scripture?

'Therefore the Lord himself will give you a sign. Look, the young woman (in Greek, a virgin) is with child and shall bear a son, and shall name him Immanuel.'

Isaiah 7. 14.

It must be stated that the idea of a virgin birth was legendary in the ancient world. There are many parallels. But I repeat that nothing appears in Mark or John or Paul … and Jesus never seems to mention it!

We can accept that Jesus' father was a carpenter and that probably Jesus followed the same trade. Incidentally, the Aramaic word can also mean a wise man or a scholar, but let us stay with carpenter. His parents were called Joseph and Mary. We have the names of his brothers … James, Joses, Judas and Simon. Mark 6.3. It is also stated that Jesus had sisters. Jesus spoke Galilean Aramaic. Hebrew was also understood and must have been used when discussing the scriptures with the Rabbis. He also probably managed some Greek as it was the language used in administration and commerce.

Jesus lived in a real world. There were priests and scribes, Pharisees and publicans, the rich and the poor, the healthy and the sick, the righteous and the sinners. They all met Jesus and they communicated with each other.

Yet he was different. Very early on in his ministry, he was seen as a prophet. 'When the chief priests and Pharisees heard his parables, they saw that he was referring to them; they wanted to arrest him, but they were afraid of the people, who looked on Jesus as a prophet.' Matthew 21. 45-46

He taught in the synagogues and in the open fields. Above all, he confronted the literal text of the law. He was remarkably direct and immediate. Everything was 'here' and 'now'. He had an 'authority' and stamped it upon those about him. He brought light into the world.

One way to attack Jesus was to insult him. He was called a bastard. The people of Nazareth had tolerated the young man, but in their eyes he was making blasphemous claims. They had to drive this apostate from his native town. What better way than to insult him with the name Jeshua ben Miriam?

Traditionally Christian dogma tells us to accept that Jesus is the son of Mary, not of Joseph. Christians go further and believe that he was begotten by an act of the Divine Creator. However, the Jews of his day saw Mary as an adulteress. Out of this came a struggle in the lifetime of Jesus ... 'Is not this the carpenter, the son of Mary?' Mark 6. 3. Again one cannot ignore the fact that neither Mark nor John mentioned the Virgin Birth and that there is no reference to it by Paul. The story did not emerge until the end of the first century.

It must be said that if there was a miraculous birth, Jesus had a head start on me. How can I be like him when he is not like me? In fact, the idea that there was a divine nature involved in the incarnation was as late as the birth stories.

I am not disparaging any of these texts, but feel that we must separate the birth of Jesus from what became the ultimate theology if we are to be comfortable with our faith. Let us look at that development. How did it evolve?

Paul is our first source of information about Jesus and was probably writing some twenty years after the death of Jesus. He was obviously deeply moved by his Christ-experience.

'We preach Christ crucified … Christ the power of God and the wisdom of God.'

1 Corinthians 1. 23-24.

Paul sees God in Christ, not divine equality or incarnation. Paul homes in on the Easter experience and apparently knows nothing of the miracle stories or of the Virgin Birth. He totally accepted the resurrection story and takes it as his basis for finding God in Christ. Even if he was aware of the Christmas saga, he does not refer to it.

There were no text books, no body of pre-conceived doctrines and no creeds in the early church. Thoughts about Jesus were not fixed and were ever changing. There was no 'faith which was once for all delivered to the saints'. Therefore we should not feel guilty about our pursuit of the 'truth'. We are allowed to question and ponder.

Forty years or so after the death of Christ, we have the Gospel of Mark. This was the first time that we have available to us a life of Jesus in chronicle form. He opens with the words … 'The beginning of the gospel (good news) of Jesus Christ … the Son of God.' He explains how these words were first heard at the baptism of Jesus by John the Baptist. The voice of God spoke from heaven … "This is my beloved son in whom I am well pleased." Paul had declared Jesus to be divine at the resurrection, Mark moves it back to the baptism, but makes little of it and the idea of divinity is not revealed until the resurrection. The Messianic secret was kept.

Some ten or twenty years later after Mark, the thoughts about the divine origins of Jesus have moved on. Matthew now produces birth stories. He quotes five passages from scripture which he correlates with the events in his story to be 'according to the scriptures'. A study of those passages shows that they were not predictions of the future, but Matthew wanted them to portray just that.

An example is that the pronouncement of the divinity is now placed in the mouth of an angel who appeared to Joseph in a dream. The divine nature was thus pre-ordained and fulfils the words of Isaiah 61.1.

'The spirit of the Lord God is upon me because the Lord has anointed me.'

Matthew traces the genealogy from David to Joseph … so how can he write that Joseph was not the father?

'A table of the descent of Jesus Christ, son of David, son of Abraham' to 'Joseph, the husband of Mary, who gave birth to Jesus called Messiah.'

Joseph was apparently descended from a good family and his birth was traced back to David, founder of the royal Jewish house.

Paul agrees with this. 'On the human level he was born of David's stock, but on the level of the spirit he was declared Son of God with full powers from the time when he rose from the dead.' Romans 1. 3.

Further, the statement of Paul who spoke about a 'spirit of holiness' is now changed by Matthew … 'Spirit of Holiness' now becomes the 'Holy Spirit'. This is hinting at the emerging doctrine of the Holy Trinity. At this point there is no mention of the Holy Spirit as a separate power. But Matthew has moved the thought on. So we are led on to the idea of the Virgin Birth induced by the 'Holy Spirit'.

Next Luke tightens up the images. He includes hymn language which reflect the Jewish Bible. The annunciating angel is given a name and appears in person and not in a dream. The annunciation was to Mary and not to Joseph, and the baby was designated as both the 'Son of God' and the 'Son of the Highest'. By the year 100 or so, Jesus' identity with God was complete and that identification is finally placed before the conception and the birth. We have moved to the pre-existence of Christ as God.

When John came to his Gospel, he omitted all birth stories even though by this time they were legion. Twice he calls Jesus the 'son of Joseph' as though he had no time for Virgin Birth stories. He probably regarded it as pagan as it was a common concept at that time.

In fact, John goes further and talks of two births as necessary … one was the natural birth and the other was the spiritual birth into the status as God's son or daughter.

'In truth, in very truth I tell you, unless a man has been born over again he cannot see the kingdom of God. "But how is it possible", said Nicodemus, "for a man to be born when he is old? Can he enter his mother's womb a second time and be born?" Jesus answered, "In truth I tell you, no one can enter the kingdom of God without being born from water and spirit. Flesh can give birth only to flesh; it is spirit that gives birth to spirit."' John 3. 4-6

Every Christmas Day the Gospel which is read at the Eucharist is John 1. 1-14 and, on every occasion, I have wondered what the congregation in the church makes of it. The language is difficult.

'When all things began, the Word (logos) already was. The Word dwelt with God, and what God was, the Word was. The Word, then, was with God at the beginning, and through him all things came to be; no single thing was created without him. All that came to be was alive with his life, and that life was the light of men. The light shines in the dark, and the darkness has never quenched it.'

John saw the 'logos' or Word, which existed in God from creation, as being born into the natural order. This is the light coming into the world. In John's Gospel, Jesus had two births … one according to the flesh of Mary and Joseph and one from the eternal 'logos'. The Greek word 'logos' describes God communicating, not just words, but himself. We are to receive the 'logos'; God is to dwell in mankind. Above all John sees Jesus as the Word … he is the light. Jesus is the Word. God is in Jesus.

Mark places the coming of the 'light' at the baptism of Jesus. Matthew traces the light coming down through the ages from Abraham to Jesus … chosen by God. Luke goes further back than Matthew to Adam … back to the creation of man.

John goes back to God in the sense that everything goes back to God. God is in Jesus and God is in mankind. This is the light that can never be extinguished. Jesus is the Word of God … Jesus is the mind of God. Another way to understand the purpose of John is to state that the mind of God became man.

The movement of thought is now complete. We talk about the pre-existence of Christ. It has become a prime concept in the Fourth Gospel. Jesus pre-existed everything.

From that point in time, the doctrines began to pile up until creeds were produced and reproduced and revised. This enabled the 'divinely appointed church' to declare the ultimate faith … accept it or be damned.

What was the point of all this? Was it to prove the divinity of Jesus? It was an attempt to make him be without sin.

The discovery of the egg cell in women in 1724 marked a dramatic leap in understanding human biology. The woman was no longer a passive receiver of the male seed, but a positive contributor in the act of procreation. The main assumption in the Virgin Birth theory was that Jesus' nature came directly from God via the Holy Spirit. Joseph was discounted. As woman was presumed to contribute nothing to human life and was regarded as purely a receptacle, immaculate conception made some sense at the time.

Many centuries were to pass before Mary was declared immaculate. Was it defined in 1854? To me that feels like last week!

The early church involved itself in controversy concerning the humanity and the divinity of Jesus and this led to an understanding of the place of the 'mother of God' in the birth of Jesus. The objective of the dispute was to state that Mary was without sin. It all seems rather contrived, although I fully accept the continuing devotion which evolved through the centuries and led to such titles as 'sinless' and 'immaculate'. Incidentally it all led inevitably to the 'Assumption of our Lady' commemorating her death … a Feast celebrating her entrance into heaven. This is a very old concept, but was made a dogma in 1950. In fact, the veneration of Mary can be traced back to the early centuries of Christianity.

> Hail Mary, full of grace,
> The Lord is with thee
> Blessed art thou among women and
> Blessed is the fruit of thy womb
> Jesus.
> Holy Mary, Mother of God
> Pray for us sinners now
> And at the hour of our death.

I find that an acceptable veneration of Mary and am content to use it in my prayer life. However, I remain puzzled as to why Jesus made no reference to his miraculous birth. Was it necessary? Jesus is my Lord and my God not because of his origin, but because of what he did and said. He draws me to God. 'I, when I am lifted up from the earth, will draw all men to myself.' Jesus is for me 'the way, the truth and the light'.

Is the Virgin Birth supposed to have put a plus to his humanity? I assume that of all creation, he as a man was sinless and that has nothing to do with his birth. He got it right! He had powers and a spiritual sensitiveness such as I cannot conceive. Dear old Peter was soundly put in his place by his master … 'You are a stumbling-block to me; you do not have in mind the things of God, but the things of men.' Matthew 16. 23. He could have been talking to me!

Dr. Barclay … an authority in understanding the Gospels … wrote: 'The Jews had a saying that in the birth of every child there were three partners, the father, the mother and the Spirit of God. They believed that no child could ever be born without the Spirit and it may well be that the New Testament stories of Jesus are lovely, poetical ways of saying that even if He had a human father, the Holy Spirit of God was operative in His birth in the most unique and special way.'

Look again at the evidence. Matthew and Luke start their stories with the suggestion that He was conceived by the Holy Spirit, which could be another way of saying that Jesus was a spirit person. Paul never mentions the family except to say that He was 'born of woman', Galatians 4. 4, and that according to the flesh he was descended from the house of David, Romans 1. 3.

Mark, the earliest Gospel, has no mention of a supernatural birth, but mentions Mary twice and not in over-flattering tones. 'Is not this the carpenter, the son of Mary, the brother of James and Joseph and Judas and Simon? Are not his sisters here with us?' Mark 6. 3. That was an insult from someone in the crowd. When He started His ministry, the family was not pleased. 'They set out to take charge of him, for the people were saying "He is out of his mind."' Mark 3. 21.

There is no great maternal love in the Gospel. Mark apparently had no knowledge of the stories of the birth of Jesus and of the sanctity of Mary.

Matthew built the virgin concept out of a mistranslation of Isaiah 7. 14 as we have seen and Luke built on it. They did their research well. The wise men came from Isaiah 60 and accounted for the camels and the gold and incense. Numbers gave us the star episode … the angel of the Lord showed the way. The shepherds came from David's association with Bethlehem … the shepherd boy who became a king. Luke actually uses a Greek word that means a 'room' rather than an inn and there is no mention of a stable. The Song of Mary … the Magnificat … is an adaptation of the song of Hannah in 1 Samuel 2. 1-10. We could go on and on.

This is all understandable. In Jesus, mankind felt the presence of God. In some way this had to be accounted for. For them God lived above the bright blue sky! Therefore there had to be a 'happening'. And they found ample sacred traditions in the scriptures to back their thoughts. We all seek an explanation for what we cannot understand.

In reality, the story brings unbelievers into our church at least once a year and we all rather enjoy the tableau that bears little reference to what is written in the Gospels. And in spite of all of that, I thoroughly enjoy Christmas. After all, all little boys are the same!

One happily accepts the position of Mary as the mother of Jesus, but I feel deep concern when she is elevated almost to the status of Jesus himself. I see no need of an intermediary …

my prayers are 'through Jesus Christ, Our Lord' and not through Mary the Mother of God.

Praying through Mary would seem to me to violate the unique position of Jesus. Her status is based upon the growth of a legend and has a questionable historical basis. Of course, we understand the need emerged to assume that Jesus had to be born of a virgin, but to use it as proof of Jesus' sinlessness is difficult to sustain and to claim that he must not be tainted by 'original sin' is questionable. It seems that the virgin birth has been created to uphold an unnecessary concept. A theory is backed up by creating facts.

Mary is not elevated as Mother of God in the Gospels, although she is cared for by Jesus on the cross and Mary was praying with the disciples on the day of Pentecost. She was firmly part of the early Jerusalem church.

And what of his family? 'He entered a house; and once more such a crowd collected round them that they had no chance to eat. When his family heard of this, they set out to take charge of him; for "He is out of his mind", they said.'
Mark 3. 20-21

All of this contradicts the birth-legends in Matthew and Luke. It must have been one of the saddest days in his life. He must have been aware of the rejection by his family and his friends in Capernaum.

'Once when great crowds were accompanying him, he turned to them and said: "If anyone comes to me and does not hate his father and mother, wife and children, brothers and sisters, even his own life, he cannot be a disciple of mine.'
Luke 14. 25.

That is an outrageous saying which must have lingered in memory.

And there is more … he refused to meet his family.

'Then his mother and his brothers arrived, and remaining outside sent in a message asking him to come out to them. A crowd was sitting round and word was brought to him: "Your mother and your brothers are outside asking for you." He replied "Who is my mother? Who are my brothers?" And looking round at those sitting in the circle about him he said, "Here are my mother and my brothers. Whoever does the will of God is my brother, my sister, my mother."

Mark 3. 31-35.

Over the centuries many theologians have attempted to water down these statements, but they remain.

Finally, it must be said that the legend of the Virgin Birth is not comparable in significance to the message of the Resurrection in primitive Christianity. The early church was well concerned with the Easter message and that was the firm message presented to the world. The growing faith in Christ had little or nothing to do with the Virgin Birth. The Easter message was paramount.

If the first two chapters of Matthew and Luke did not exist, I do not think that my concept of the Christ would be any different. My faith would be no different. God is revealed to me in Jesus Christ.

However the story has found its way into the Christian creeds. We are stuck with it! But in spite of all previous thoughts, I find it possible in church to use the formulation 'conceived by the Holy Spirit, born of the Virgin Mary'. I understand the intention of that statement and how it was an attempt to explain the being of Jesus. Above all, I accept that Jesus' origin was a human event truly blessed by God in every way.

Three hundred years were to pass before we have what we call the Nicene Creed. It tones down the human experience of Jesus. The language is exalted in favour of Jesus' divinity, saying that he is 'the only Son of God, eternally begotten of the Father, God from God, Light from Light, true God from true God, begotten, not made, of one being with the Father.' Only then do we go on to confirm that 'he came down from heaven, and became incarnate of the Virgin Mary and was made man.' His humanity comes in a poor second place to his divinity. This continued down through the centuries and the human Christ was almost forgotten.

And, of course, there will be a crib in my home with all the trimmings … 'love came down at Christmas' and comes into my life.

Chapter Five

WHAT KIND OF MAN AM I?

At the tail end of 1956, I was appointed to the staff of Llandaff Cathedral in Cardiff. The Cathedral had been 'gutted' by the Luftwaffe in 1941 and my arrival in the Cathedral coincided with the completion of the restoration. The architect, George Pace, had worked wonders with the building. Happily most of the over-ornate Victorian additions had been removed by Hitler and this resulted in an open vista and a sense of space. A John Piper window glowed with glorious colour and added to the aura of light and beauty. It was an exciting time.

An episode stands out in my memory.

There was a rather important addition which had not arrived … Epstein's Majestas. The whole place was closed to the public as the final cosmetics were accomplished by a group of volunteers. There was much polishing and dusting, carrying of chairs and books and general bustle with a purpose. Then the Majestas appeared as planned.

The organ was being tuned with odd burbles and explosions of sound. Workmen scurried with intent. I sat quietly in the back row of the nave, observing all this organised frenzy. Alongside me sat Jacob Epstein. He chatted away, asking questions, rubbing his hands, rocking back and fore; it dawned upon me that this great man was nervous. I was struck dumb! What could I possibly say that might be of interest to this man! We were well matched, one a bit twitchy, the other with a stammer.

The conversation improved. He talked of the work of a Cathedral as he saw it. He asked about the people and the congregation, their ideas of artistic expression and whether they would see what he could see and understand as he understood. He was really worried about his Majestas.

As we chatted, we watched the seventeen feet of unpolished aluminium being hoisted and fixed on to the overhead drum of the Pulpitum, above the chancel steps. Epstein stopped talking. We just gazed.

For the first time I saw Christ as Epstein saw Christ. Truly it was majestic.

The face seemed to shine as it looked heavenward and away from where we sat. It was as though Christ saw that the final journey for mankind was that we were to be 'absorbed' into the awesome presence of God. I was looking at the King of Kings going home. It was the face of the Transfiguration.

The arms hung down with the hands open towards those who dared to look. They seemed to beckon and strain to lift each one of us. These were the hands come down from the Cross to call mankind to enter the Kingdom, which Christ had made ours. Here was the strength of Christ made visible to man. Words were not needed. The invitation was not just to follow, but to be lifted up and make the journey to God, supported by the hands of Christ.

My eyes came down along the elongated robes to the hanging feet, which still carried the marks of the nails, the evidence of all the pain and suffering of mankind. I realised that the pain and suffering was also given to God.

As my eyes returned to that majestic face, I realised that I was in a place where man had come to worship for a thousand years and that this Majestas could remain there for another thousand.

By this time the organ was at full thunder and we both sat, wrapped in thought. Then, at last, he turned to me.

"Well?"

I stumbled to express my emotions. I told him what I could see. He made little comment, but seemed to listen. Later with the foolishness of youth and probably because we had sat so long together, I questioned him about the mechanics of creating such a work, and then went in feet first.

"Was it difficult for you, a practising Jew, to create a Christ for a Christian congregation?"

It was a natural question and I can recall almost his exact words.

"All my life I have searched for truth and beauty and, in the end, I discovered that it is in the idea of the Christ that they are to be found."

That was the climax of our conversation. I was never given the chance to speak to Epstein again. As the years have passed, his words have taken on a deeper meaning. I have discussed them with many people from many nations and theologies.

Whatever your religion or lack of it, every man has to create for himself his own ideas of truth and beauty. They may not seem to be of much worth to others, but without a vision man has no place to go and life becomes just a repetitive drudge. We all need the idea of a King ... and many of us dream of His Kingdom being right here on earth.

It had been an encounter with a great man.

Jesus had such an encounter and was faced with the question … "What kind of man am I?" We might think that we can supply the answer … God-man or the Son of God or Christ or the Messiah of God.

It had all started when Jesus decided to join up with John the Baptist in the upper regions of Galilee, which was a hot-bed of political disturbance. The Jews there were all intent on overthrowing the Roman yoke. The insurgents were called the Zealots and many of them were to be crucified. No wonder the family thought that Jesus was deranged, mixing with such rabble.

The two men, Jesus and John, were related through their mothers, but whether they met as children we do not know. Surely the family would have chatted about John who was earning a reputation for asceticism, holiness of life and for his boldness of speech.

John was a tough character used to living rough in an uncompromising environment. Jesus was to be described by some as a glutton and wine-bibber … John the Baptist was the opposite. John wore a goat's hair coat and fed on locusts and wild-honey. He was an impressive figure and had a large following of disciples, but was eventually to be murdered judiciously. He had taught that there was a Kingdom coming and that his followers were to prepare for it by exercising all the virtues … his message was simple, 'Repent and be better Jews'!

Jesus' encounter with John was a turning point. Jesus was excited by the message of his cousin who was proclaiming the coming of the Kingdom of God … it was food for thought. 'Thy Kingdom come, thy will be done, on earth as it is in heaven' would sum up the prayer of every Jew … it was a cry from the heart. Jesus must have been deeply moved by his cousin. The message was clear. Repent and be baptised was the way into the kingdom. We have lost the real meaning of the Greek word 'metanoia' … repentance. It means an utter change of life, heart and soul and, above all, the abandoning of your present life and a complete commitment to God. This was the challenge for Jesus. Let Mark tell the story.

'In the prophet Isaiah it stands written: 'Here is my herald whom I send on ahead of you, and he will prepare your way. A voice crying aloud in the wilderness, "Prepare a way for the Lord; clear a straight path for him." And so it was that John the Baptist appeared in the wilderness proclaiming a baptism in token of repentance, for the forgiveness of sins; and they flocked to him from the whole Judean countryside and the city of Jerusalem, and were baptised by him in the River Jordan, confessing their sins.

John was dressed in a rough coat of goat's hair, with a leather belt round his waist, and he fed on locusts and wild honey. His proclamation ran: 'After me comes one who is mightier than I. I am not fit to unfasten his shoes. I have baptised you with water; he will baptise you with the Holy Spirit.'

It happened at this time that Jesus came from Nazareth in Galilee and was baptised in the Jordan by John. At the moment when he came up out of the water, he saw the heavens torn open and the Spirit, like a dove, descending upon him. And a voice spoke from heaven: 'Thou art my Son, my Beloved; on thee my favour rests.'

Thereupon the Spirit sent him away into the wilderness, and there he remained for forty days tempted by Satan.'
Mark 1. 2-12.

This was the beginning of the mission of Jesus. There was much to think about. We call it the 'Temptations'.

When, some time later, John was in prison, he had doubts about Jesus and sent some of his followers to ask, 'Are you the one who was to come or should we expect someone else?' The answer was, 'Go back and tell him the blind receive sight, the lame walk, those who have leprosy are cured, the deaf hear, the dead are raised and the good news is preached to the poor.' This must have puzzled John who had expected much more from a Messiah.

John the Baptist was looking for signs that the Messiah would come to lift the Roman yoke. The message of Jesus was not what he had expected. Jesus was obviously talking about a Kingdom not of this world, but based upon virtue and love. 'The Kingdom of God is within you.' It was even worse. There were rumours that Jesus was 'a glutton and a drunkard, a friend of tax collectors and sinners'. One wonders whether John was disappointed in his cousin.

The early followers of Jesus also must have hoped that

he was the Messiah. The word 'Messiah' is a Hebrew word which translated into Greek is 'Christ'. Many Jews expected the Messiah to be a political leader who would overthrow the Roman rule. The Old Testament has many images portraying the coming of such a Messiah.

After the baptism by John, Jesus faced the temptations in the desert. He was well used to the desert as he had spent much time with John the Baptist and his followers. He had tasted the life of the ascetic. But there must be another way. The temptations were not asking Jesus to prove his divinity, but asking, 'What kind of man are you?' 'What am I to do?'

Jesus must have discussed his desert experiences with his disciples. The first temptation is classically simple. Turn stones into bread. Feed the people and you will be a popular person. Jesus had probably been meditating on Deuteronomy 8. 3 … he was well steeped in the scriptures.

'He humbled you and made you hungry; then he fed you on manna … to teach you that man cannot live on bread alone but lives by every word that comes from the mouth of the Lord.'

Bread is not enough … change the hearts of mankind! 'What am I to do' was being answered.

The second temptation was almost bizarre … throw yourself over a cliff and let the Lord your God save you. That would surely prove that God was with you. Again when he discussed all of this with his disciples, he quoted from Deuteronomy 6. 16.

'You must not challenge (better translation of the Greek is 'test') the Lord your God … you must diligently keep the commandments of the Lord your God.'

It would have been spectacular, but would have proved nothing. Once again 'What am I to do' was being answered … 'love God and love your neighbour' is the entry code for the Kingdom.

The third temptation was the toughest. Matthew 4. 8-9. The power of evil says: 'All this I will give you, if you bow down and worship me.' That would be power indeed! He could free his people from the Roman occupation. He could be an important politician. The people even suggested that he could be an earthly king. But he was to forbid people from even calling him 'master'. I suspect that he had no ambition to found a new religion. It was enough for him to call God Father … his creator. And surely Jesus would have been surprised that he did in fact father the pomp and pomposity of what we have today in our form of Christianity. Jesus knew and accepted the fact that he was to teach the road to inner virtue … we are to walk with God and that is enough. Anything more than that is to give in to the third temptation.

There is one passage in Deuteronomy which makes sense of the temptation episode and possibly was used by Jesus when he talked to his disciples about the whole experience. Moses is depicted to be addressing the Israelites after their escape from Egypt and it is recorded in Deuteronomy 8. 2.

'You must remember all that road by which the Lord your God has led you these forty years in the wilderness to humble you, to test you and to discover whether or no it was in your heart to keep his commandments.'

In Judaism the number 'forty' was the traditional time to test your vocation. 'Jesus was led by the Spirit, into the wilderness, to be tempted (the same Greek word for 'test'), and he fasted forty days and forty nights.' Matthew 4. 1, Mark 1. 12, and Luke 4. 1.

Let us weigh these thoughts against the way of life that he chose. In some ways he succumbed to the temptations as though he could not help himself. He did feed the hungry. Most of the healing miracles would appear to occur as the result of pure compassion. He could not pass on the other side when he saw human need and misery. He invariably told the recipients not to tell anyone because it was of no benefit for mankind. He knew that it would not be the way. Miracles proved nothing.

He started his ministry in Galilee. It was a green place, a lush area, ideal for agriculture. It huddled around the inland Sea of Galilee. Above all, the fishing was good and there was a steady trade with Jerusalem. Politically, it was somewhat independent and rather separated from the control of Jerusalem. The north end of Galilee was a hot-bed of rebellion against the Roman conqueror … it was the home of the Zealots.

'Very early the next morning he got up and went out. He went away to a lonely spot and remained there in prayer. But Simon and his companions searched him out, found him, and said, 'They are all looking for you.' He answered, 'Let us move out to the country towns in the neighbourhood; I have to proclaim my message there also; that is what I came out to do.'

Mark 1. 35-38.

Matthew 4. 23–25 paints the picture. 'Jesus went throughout Galilee teaching in their synagogues, preaching the good news of the kingdom, and healing every disease and sickness among the people. News about him spread all over Syria, and people brought him all who were ill of various diseases.'

This Kingdom business was hard, tiring work. The crowds followed and the more he did, the more was expected. If you jump off a cliff and survive, there are those who missed it. If you miss the trick of the conjuror, you ask him to do it over and over again. He was tired.

We read that he went into a boat to get away from the crowds and to rest and the disciples took the craft off the shore whilst he slept. The story continues.

'A heavy squall came on and the waves broke over the boat until it was all but swamped. Now he was in the stern asleep on a cushion; they roused him and said, "Master, we are sinking! Do you not care?" He stood up, rebuked the wind, and said to the sea, "Hush! Be still!" The wind dropped and there was a dead calm. He said to them, "Why are you such cowards? Have you no faith even now?" They were awestruck and said to one another, "Who can this be whom even the wind and the sea obey?"'

Mark 4. 37-41.

'Jesus then got into the boat, and his disciples followed. All at once a great storm arose on the lake, till the waves were breaking right over the boat; but he went on sleeping. So they came and woke as him up, crying "Save us, Lord; we are sinking!" "Why are you such cowards?" he said; "how little faith you have!" Then he stood up and rebuked the wind and the sea, and there was a dead calm. The men were astonished at

what had happened, and exclaimed, "What sort of man is this, that even the wind and the sea obey him?"'
Matthew 8. 23-27.

'One day he got into a boat with his disciples and said to them, "Let us cross over to the other side of the lake." So they put out; and as they sailed along he went to sleep. Then a heavy squall struck the lake; they began to ship water and were in grave danger. They went to him, and roused him, crying, "Master, Master, we are sinking!" He awoke, and rebuked the wind and the turbulent waters. The storm subsided and all was calm. "Where is your faith?" he asked. In fear and astonishment they said to one another, "Who can this be? He gives his orders to wind and waves, and they obey him."'
Luke 8. 22-25

The 'stilling of the storm'.

Chatting aboard a very small Irish coaster, the MARIZELL, when I was the Port Chaplain of Liverpool, this story came into the conversation. I talked about the power that Jesus had over nature. The Captain, Barry Tyrell, said "I believe they have misinterpreted what actually happened." He began to explain his thoughts. The Irish Sea provided a full gale every week in winter and the waters often swept over the top of the Bridge. Barry Tyrell was no stranger to storms at sea. "These men were professionals" said Barry. "But it sounds as though they lost their nerve!" Jesus was talking to them. 'Keep calm! Have faith in yourselves!' Jesus had said the right thing to them. It was enough and the rigours of the storm were manageable.

That made a lot of sense to me. How often when the storm breaks over us do we get it wrong! To pray for a miracle to help and cure a loved one is natural, but probably entirely wrong. Why should I expect God to discriminate in favour of one soul against another? That is not an act of love. It is an act of selfishness … even though it is understandable. Our prayer should be that our loved ones should have faith and courage so that whatever storms befall them, there may be peace and stillness in their hearts. Pray for peace in your heart. That is love. That is the miracle.

Jesus knew that if you can walk with God, the storms of life are not threatening and we can cope with them. Keep your faith. Sadly, the pain remains.

What difference would it make to me in my life if Jesus had stilled that storm? What would it prove to me about Jesus? My answer is that it would not matter to me at all. The punch line is that Jesus has no need to still the tempests in your life, but he must enable you to cope with them. You have to face the tempests head-on in the same way that a Master of a ship does. You cannot run away from a storm, you have to face it head-on. You cannot run away from problems. I need Him to say to me 'Keep calm! Hold the faith and all will be well.' It is worth repeating the thought. Jesus does not need to still the waves, he needs to still me. That is the real miracle and that was the mission of Jesus. It is called love. It is Kingdom business.

The Gospel writers as ever were intent on proving the divinity of Jesus and surely missed the punch line. Jesus was concerned with love, not stilling storms. Take the thought a little further. Luke makes a fascinating remark. 'Why callest thou me good? None is good, save one that is God.' Another translation of the Greek says, 'No one is good, except God alone.' Luke: 18. 19. Jesus did not claim to be sinless. Jesus stated, 'It is the Father, living in me, who is doing his work. Anyone who has faith in me will do what I have been doing.' He saw God at work in man. Jesus is prepared to stand along side each one of us and will work through us and within us until mankind fulfils God's will. What is important is the fact that Jesus can be 'in us'. The message is that Jesus can be with us every step of our lives. That is the miracle. The will of God can be fulfilled through me. Whatever happens, God is with me. That is a tremendous thought. That is the stilling of the storm.

Walking on water does not prove divinity. What you should say is, 'Do you mind showing me how you can do that?' Of course, there are endless jokes about stepping stones! It is the 'falling off the cliff' syndrome ... clever stuff, but 'do it again'. I have heard all the funny stories.

Healing a leper ... never mind how it is done ... was not done by Jesus to prove his divinity. Jesus loved lepers and he knew how to make them well. Incidentally, we can cure leprosy these days and I like to think that we also do it because we love lepers and want them to be well. Unfortunately, most of what Jesus did was written up and exaggerated and gilded and I suspect that we attribute to him what he would not claim himself. Surely, he was indicating that in this Kingdom of his, this is what you do. If you have looked into the face of a person eaten up with cancer, you will know that you must show your love for them … and it is not easy. I want to accept that all of his actions were expressions of his love for us. That is what the Kingdom is all about. In fact you can judge his life and yours against the word 'love'. 'Love came down at Christmas' is about right … that surely is what happened.

Healing a leper is pure love. Turning one hundred and twenty gallons of water into wine … a story in one Gospel only and written fifty years after the event … fills me full of doubt. Every parson gets his leg pulled about this and we all smile. And I too join in the nonsense, because nothing important hangs on this supposed miracle. It proves little.

If you are looking for a punch line in the miracle business, try this. Jesus had the desire to serve men and to love mankind and show them the way into the Kingdom of God. However, I do not need a miracle to prove His worth for me. The greatest wonder is the fact that Jesus came into this world and by walking with him alongside me, I can receive his grace (divine help). In this way he can change lives. The punch line is 'You need never walk alone'. Coming from Liverpool I even have my anthem … with no apologies!

When you walk through the storm
Hold your head up high
And don't be afraid of the dark.
At the end of the storm
Is a golden sky
And the sweet silver song of a lark.
Walk on through the wind

Walk on through the rain
Though your dreams be tossed and blown;
Walk on, walk on with hope in your heart
And you'll never walk alone.
You'll never walk alone.

This is a religion that I can work with.

An old, seafaring friend presented me with a ship in a bottle. It is beautifully done and a proud possession. His name was Captain Johns. Between the wars he was tramping in the Far East looking for cargo when the days were hard. He drank whisky, and filled his days of boredom by putting ships into bottles. He was never short of bottles and became an expert at his art. He was a character who smoked a smelly pipe with his teeth out … when I think about it, they were always out!

Some of us see our religion like a ship in a bottle. It is safe and secure, there is nothing to disturb it and nothing can ever change. It must not be questioned or you will be accused of blasphemy. Do not question … believe. It shelters the pious and the favoured from the risks that others have to face. But life is not like that … and neither is a ship. A ship is made to travel far and wide over the horizon; a ship is made to go into the unknown, to take risks and to face the world head-on. A ship cannot be contained in a bottle!

And so it must be with your faith. For almost fifty years I have worked with seafarers of all colour and creed and nationality. I have been challenged and disparaged and there have been seemingly endless storms and tempests in my life. I needed courage, cheerfulness and strength in order to survive in the world that was mine. No-one said that it would be easy. The miracle was that, almost without thinking, I more than survived. It can be done. And here is how it is done. You never walk alone.

The Gospel writers used their knowledge of the scriptures. After the Stilling of the Storm, the disciples said to each other, 'Who is this? Even the wind and the waves obey him!' For them only God had power over the wind and the waves. 'They saw the works of the Lord, his wonderful deeds in the deep.' Psalm 107 carries the story

'Then they cried out to the Lord in their trouble,
And he brought them out of their distress.
He stilled the storm to a whisper;
The waves of the sea were hushed.
They were glad when it grew calm,
And he guided them to their desired haven.'

The connection between the Stilling of the Storm and this Psalm would have been obvious to the gospel writers. Jesus was fulfilling scripture. That surely is why they missed the punch line in this miracle. You might accuse me of avoiding acceptance of this miracle and turning it into a 'comfort story'! Incidentally, look up the word 'comfort' in a dictionary ... it means 'to strengthen completely'. And that is exactly what Jesus did to those disciples

The danger of seeing the miracles and the life of Jesus as Jesus acting out a role as though every action was organised by him to make a point matched by a scriptural reference is that you are stating that he willed it all to happen. It was all pre-ordained. The gospel writers did just that. His life had to be 'according to the scriptures'. Are you saying that he deliberately put his life at risk, he organised his arrest and trial and death? It is as though he was committing suicide according to the scriptures and was playing out the whole scene. That seems improbable and I cannot accept it.

My thoughts are is that his family had no idea of his divinity; his mother did not understand and most concluded that he was crazy. At no point does Jesus himself claim an unusual birth. He lived and died like one of us. There certainly was endless argument as to whether he was the Messiah or not, but he was not seen as a god descended upon earth … he was a carpenter's son.

Our picture of Christ is emerging. There is a Christ of post-Easter … he is painted as divine … one might describe him as the 'Jesus of faith'. This naturally is the Jesus that I was taught about as a child and he has remained with me all these years. This is the 'gentle Jesus meek and mild' syndrome.

But now there is another Christ … a man from Nazareth … and he, too, is shaping and guiding me. He is a vibrant figure. He is a man of action and contradictions; he performs strange deeds. He is free from evil and wickedness and lives a life in complete harmony with God. He is a person who draws me to him and I want to follow him as those who knew him did.

Sadly, I think that two thousand years later we have built a plastic Christ, who fits in remarkably well with the over-pretty pictures and images we find in so many of our churches. It is a little bit like living with the painted wise men and shepherds of Christmas day, with a figure of a westernised Mary and with all the reality of Coronation Street on television. We fill our churches with unreal statues, the gold and tinsel of inferior art and are surprised when our lay people dismiss us as irrelevant. We are failing our people. We clergy dress up in strange garb and our pontiffs claim ancestry with this clouded past. I am too old to be moved by all this ecclesiastical baggage, which I have carried for over eighty years.

Of course it has helped me along the way, and I still need the fellowship of those who worship, but I welcome the freedom of thought that has come with age. The Jesus I believe in is beyond all belief and in truth my faith is too small to grasp the wonder of this person who, at long last, has come into my life.

I believe in Jesus, my Lord. Think about Doubting Thomas. He cut through all the mists of doubt and simply said, 'You are my Lord and my God.' And that was it. At last, I am free of the baggage of the passing years. I have found a Jesus I can live with.

Chapter Six

MIRACLES AND THINGS

Jesus spent much of his time in Galilee, the northern part of the country where he grew up. He came south a number of times with possibly a few visits to Jerusalem. He was a teacher and a miracle worker and lived within the Jewish world in the first century.

His natural home was the Galilean town of Capernaum … he called it his own city. There is little left of it now. At the north end of the Sea of Galilee, the fast running river Jordan tumbles into the lake. Dark eucalyptus trees and tufts of grass growing within the white flagstones and four pillars … that is all that remains of the one-time splendid synagogue. Southward over the lake was Jerusalem high in the blue hills. There are now no synagogues left from the time of Jesus. The Romans in two bloody wars razed Jerusalem to the ground and the inhabitants of that ancient city were scattered to the four winds.

'Then they came to Capernaum, and on the Sabbath he went to synagogue and began to preach. The people were astounded at his teaching.' Mark 1. 21.

Most of the inhabitants lived on the natural riches of the lake; their little houses nestled in numbers on the gentle slope of the lake and around the synagogue. It was at the edge of these waters that he took his first decisive step towards proclaiming his message.

'Jesus was walking by the shore of the Sea of Galilee when he saw Simon and his brother Andrew on the lake at work with a casting net; for they were fishermen. Jesus said to them, "Come with me, and I will make you fishers of men." And at once they left their nets and followed him.' Mark 1. 16-18

When he had gone a little further he saw James the son of Zebedee and his brother John, who were in the boat overhauling their nets. He called them; and leaving their father Zebedee in the boat, they went off to follow him. I suspect that they were old friends.

Jesus would have often wandered into the Galilean hills, and preached in many of the towns and villages, but he always returned to the little fishing town; it remained the main centre of his mission. One day he was to leave Capernaum and set out with his twelve disciples for Jerusalem … it was his last journey.

The Jews believed that their God was the only God and all others were idols and of no value. Jesus believed this. He believed that he was a prophet and that his message was to announce the coming of the 'Kingdom of God'. Living under the heel of Rome must surely have given that phrase political overtones. We could build a story around that thought. 'Jesus was a Jewish revolutionary'. He announced the Kingdom of God and gathered his followers about. They marched to Jerusalem and there he died … just another failed revolutionary! After all, his cousin, John the Baptist had done just that and was beheaded for his trouble. But for Jesus that was not the way.

His Kingdom was different and we shall find his

thoughts about that Kingdom in his life and teaching. His Kingdom was for all people and that was new and that would cost him his life.

Most of his teaching was in parables … earthly stories with a heavenly meaning … they were really simple stories about everyday life. He talked to ordinary people in a language that they understood. We all remember the Good Samaritan who looked after a stranger, the lost sheep found by a shepherd who cared for him, the prodigal son who came home to say sorry, the unmerciful servant who didn't do to others what had been done to him. All of his stories had understandable punch lines.

Then there were the miracles. He fed 5,000 people with a few loaves and a couple of fish, he walked on water and stilled the waves, he appeared in glory to his disciples, and he raised Lazarus from the dead. People did not know what to make of him. Some said that he was a prophet or that he was a past prophet returned to life. They were puzzled as they wondered if he was the Messiah who would liberate them from the Roman rule. Was this to be the man who would set up a Kingdom and make the nation free?

Jesus once took Peter, James and John to a quiet place and was transformed … transfigured … in front of their eyes. "That's what I am!" he said. "I am God's Son from heaven, not a soldier on earth." I suspect that they had little idea what he was telling them.

The ordinary folk were often offended because he seemed to despise the old traditions which they had always accepted with little thought. He wanted to alter God's law! So he was dismissed as a trickster and false teacher. He was attacking what had been taught for generations.

The trouble was that some people, who had really watched him and listened to him, were to be never the same again. Decades later he was to be described as the man who turned the world upside down.

And that is why I too want to look again and listen and come to my own conclusion as to what manner of man this was.

The disciples had been with him for many months, the crowds were growing bigger every day. Already he was getting into trouble … the Pharisees and the Sadducees had no time for his teaching and on top of that his cousin, John the Baptist, after months in prison had been executed by King Herod. Life was hard.

The disciples were happy to embark on a boat at the Sea of Galilee to find some peace and quiet. It was not to be. The crowds followed the boat around the coast and as they touched land, they were waiting for him to speak. He was worth listening to. The crowd was large and he stayed on the boat to teach.

It is unlikely that the Gospels contain his exact words. What we read would not have been spoken in one go, but spread over many occasions and later collected and remembered and collated. Sayings about the Kingdom would have been accumulated. Such would have been the Sermon on the Mount. It is wonderful to read.

He expanded the teaching of the day. "It's not enough to keep the letter of the law. The prophets told us not to kill, I tell you not to be angry or argue or carry hatred in your heart. If someone hits you on the right cheek, turn the other so they can strike that too. Do not hate your enemies. You should be kind and loving to all."

This was amazing stuff to absorb. The crowds were enthralled. He talked about building a house on rock and not on sand. They understood that. Do your fasting in secret, and give to charity in secret … your reward will be in heaven and not in the adulation of your fellow men. This teaching was different and they were to remember it.

So Jesus taught and they listened and remembered … and many decades after the event they wrote it down.

I happily concede that some folk regard every word and letter of the Bible as written by the hand of God. It is their privilege to think that, although I have to add that they should start with the Greek text as opposed to the archaic English so beloved by so many. In reality, we are not even certain as to which Greek text is original or possibly that we even have an original text! And do remember that Jesus probably taught and spoke in Aramaic.

But let us look at some miracles and start with the fourth miracle … the feeding of the five thousand. It is well documented and is the only miracle that appears in all four Gospels. John 6. 5-14; Matthew 14. 15-21; Mark 6. 33-44; and Luke 9. 12-17.

They all record the same story although like any reporting there are differences in details. John's account is the latest and he has a firm theological approach to this miracle.

John saw the miracles as 'signs' of his divinity. He recorded the miraculous to prove that Jesus was God.

Most of us are familiar with this miracle. The disciples were concerned about the crowds as the evening approached. It was time for them to go home and eat. Jesus asked Philip, "Where shall we buy bread for all these people?" Philip virtually replied, "Eight month's wages would not buy enough bread for each to have a bite!" At this point, Andrew spoke up, "Here is a boy with five small barley loaves and two small fish, but how far will they go among so many?" Jesus said, "Make them sit down." There followed the feeding of the five thousand.

What really happened? Something did happen and it was well talked about and remembered. What did happen on the shores of Galilee two thousand years ago?

My worries over the years are all about logistics … not a word I love! How is it possible for one man to take a small bundle of food, break it and divide it and have it distributed amongst five thousand folk, all sitting higgledy-piggledy on the grass? Think about it. It would have taken hours. The people on the edge of the gathering would not have a clue that bread and fish were on the way to them. I fail to see how it could have been achieved. It would not have been practical. It was physically impossible. So what did happen? Something did. Let's look again.

Read again that John records the presence of that lad with the fish and bread. 'Andrew, the brother of Simon Peter, said to him, "There is a boy here, who has five barley loaves and two fishes; but what is that among so many". John 6. 9.

Think about it. The mother of that boy made sure that he had food and drink before he set out that day. No-one organises a Sunday school ramble without making certain that provisions are available. There must have been tons of food and drink tucked away in the haversacks of that five thousand. No mother worth her salt would have had it otherwise. There was a super abundance of food.

This miracle is not about creating food. There was more than enough. At the end of the tale, we read that many baskets of food were left over! They actually state that there were twelve baskets of food left over … rather a symbolic number that … enough for the twelve tribes of Israel. One supposes that if there were ten tribes of Israel, there would have been ten baskets left over! Or was the story suggesting that there was enough food for each of the twelve apostles to feed the world? Take your pick. Such is editing!

The miracle that was needed on the shore of Galilee was to shame them into sharing their bounty amongst their neighbours. That to me is a far greater miracle than performing magic with the fish and the bread. Jesus was concerned with the changing of people's lives. That makes sense to me. Jesus came to stir us into action and that needs a miracle. Here was the man who turned the world upside down … in action.

The accounts we have are well tinkered and tortured to prove the wonder works of Jesus. The real truth of what happened has been well 'baggaged' and wrapped up. The fact was that there was plenty of food available. The stupidity of man was the stumbling block and Jesus shamed them into action. That was the miracle on the shore of Galilee. It was so simple a message that it was missed in order to 'prove' the divinity of Jesus.

The idea that Jesus performed this miracle on the hearts of that crowd is not original, but I would rather teach a class of youngsters that this man Jesus could transform the greedy and selfish into sharing their bounty than indulging in some sleight of hand with bread and fish.

The message for mankind today is that there is more than enough food in this world. There should be no starvation. We need Jesus on television to shame us into caring for and loving our neighbours. European mountains of butter or whatever are an insult to each one of us. We truly should be ashamed of ourselves.

Of course, we need the miracle of the feeding of the five thousand. Jesus tells us that this is the way in which you must behave in the Kingdom of God. It is one of the rules … 'Love each other'. It is a Kingdom miracle.

But why did Jesus indulge in miracles? It might help us to understand if we remember that his main concern was to communicate the Kingdom of God as a vibrant possibility. The connection between the miracles and the Kingdom is not easily transparent. He healed people by being touched on the hem of his garment, and he used his saliva to give sight to the blind. Jesus cured folk. And that in most cases was all that was seen. Jesus was a healer and an exorcist casting out demons.

These healing miracles are impressive. I was taught

that Jesus performed miracles because he was deeply moved with compassion for the sick and the needy, but there is more to it than that.

'So Jesus went round all the towns and villages teaching in their synagogues, announcing the good news of the Kingdom and curing every kind of ailment and disease.' Matthew 9. 35

His main intention was to signify that the Kingdom was dawning and his actions were symbols of what that Kingdom was about.

'Jesus said, "Accept the evidence of my deeds, even if you do not believe me."' John 10. 38

Thirty-five miracles are attributed to Jesus, handed down in Aramaic and kept alive by the story tellers. Many critics have tried to ignore the miracles as though they did not happen and then presume that what was left in the Gospels was the authentic story of Jesus. That is a modern approach, but in the days of Jesus all miracles would have been accepted as the normal practice of a prophet. I fully accept that Jesus performed miracles, but not as written.

Go back again to the miracle of the loaves and fishes. It is uncertain whether there were five loaves and two fishes and five thousand people or seven loaves and a few fish to four thousand. There are six accounts of the episode in the four Gospels. The writers use the miracle in different ways to make their points.

John reflects on the bread sent down from heaven to Moses. 'I tell you this: the truth is, not that Moses gave you bread from heaven. The bread that God gives comes down from heaven and brings life to the world.' John 6. 32. That is part of John's interpretation of the miracle.

Other quotations link the story firmly to the Eucharist, which was not in existence at the time of the miracle and therefore can only be a hindsight-commentary.

The miracle was invested with a profound spiritual significance, which is pure hindsight by each writer. In fact, they missed the whole point of what happened on the shores of Galilee. I believe that Jesus merely was enacting the simple basic Kingdom rule that you must share all things with your neighbour ... it is called 'loving your neighbour'.

But surely the biggest problem that we have with miracles is when we read that he made the dead live. That really is a miracle!

The most 'impossible' miracle is the raising of Lazarus from the dead. John 11. 1-44. The first problem is that John treats the miracles in his own way. Like the other Gospel writers he sees them as much more than mere wonders ... he gives them a deep spiritual meaning. He records seven miracles and they are each recorded as an example of the 'power' of Jesus. John says that a miracle is a 'sign' of that power. The Lazarus story is firmly recorded as the precursor of the Resurrection. It is a sign of what is to come.

Let's sidetrack for a moment. The nearest gospel story to John's Lazarus story is the parable of Dives (the rich man) and Lazarus. It is a parable .... an earthly story with a heavenly meaning. The moral of that parable is that if the Jews did not listen to Moses and the prophets, they will pay no heed even if someone should rise from the dead.

Here is the Dives and Lazarus parable. Luke16. 19-31.

'There was once a rich man, who dressed in purple and the finest linen, and feasted in great magnificence every day. At his gate, covered with sores, lay a poor man Lazarus, who would have been glad to satisfy his hunger with the scraps from the rich man's table. Even the dogs used to come and lick his sores. One day the poor man died and was carried away by the angels to be with Abraham. The rich man also died and was buried, and in Hades, where he was in torment, he looked up; and there, far away, was Abraham with Lazarus close beside him. "Abraham, my father," he called out, "take pity on me! Send Lazarus to dip the tip of his finger in water, to cool my tongue, for I am in agony in this fire." But Abraham said, "Remember, my child, that all the good things fell to you while you were alive, and all the bad to Lazarus; now he has his consolation here and it is you who are in agony. But that is not all: there is a great chasm fixed between us; no one from our side who wants to reach you can cross it, and none may pass from your side to us." "Then, father," he replied, "will you send him to my father's house, where I have five brothers, to warn them, so that they too may not come to this place of torment?" But Abraham said, "They have Moses and the prophets; let them listen to them." "No, father Abraham," he replied, "but if someone from the dead visits them, they will repent." Abraham answered, "If they do not listen to Moses and the prophets they will pay no heed even if someone should rise from the dead."'

In John's Gospel this parable has become a literal event. Lazarus does in fact rise from the dead, and the Jews are not persuaded. John then takes it much further … the importance is not the event, but the meaning which is the resurrection of Jesus that restores humanity into new life. If John's miracle story actually happened, it seems impossible for the other Gospel writers to have ignored it unless they were unaware of it.

John writes that Lazarus had been dead for four days and corruption had already set in. "Unbind him and let him go," says Jesus. Symbolically, free mankind from the bondage of death. The sign in John means that Jesus has power over death. In John it is no longer a 'kingdom' story.

Luke had made it a kingdom story … the Jews will find it hard to enter the kingdom! John made it a 'sign' that Jesus has power over death and it was a fore-runner of the resurrection.

Perhaps we must accept that it came from a pre-Lucan source and came into the tradition at a later date and was not known by the three Gospel writers. All that we can state is that John takes it for granted that it really happened and he saw it as a 'sign' of the power of Jesus.

Personally I believe that a 'kingdom' story had been upgraded by the passage of time into a 'power' story. At no point do I deny that Jesus had miraculous power, but I still ask a simple question, 'What really happened?'

Let's play a game. Dunkirk is rather a long time ago … in terms of time just about the span between the living Jesus and the Gospel writers.

We know what happened at Dunkirk. It was a time of intense trauma. The Nazis had over-run Europe and France was defeated. Our army was trapped on the beach at Dunkirk, fighting a rear-guard action for survival. Then the miracle! Little ships crossed from Britain and the British expeditionary force was ferried back to the mainland. It was a remarkable action and at the time it was seen as a victory and not a defeat.

Move Dunkirk back two thousand years and the story would have been told in a different way. God would have guided the entire scenario. 'The hand of God came upon the face of the waters and there was a great calm and by the power of God the little army was brought home to safety and by the grace of God, in time, it was to defeat the powers of evil.' In truth for many at the time, that was the way it seemed to be.

Today we still talk about the miracle of Dunkirk. Yet to many Frenchmen, it is still seen as an abandonment of their cause and a cowardly retreat by the British. For many it was regarded as a misjudgement by Hitler as he missed the opportunity to overcome the British. For many in the world, including the American ambassador in London, it was the end of Britain and the death of the British Empire. We were defeated. If it was a miracle, its nature is rather obscure. It all depends upon your point of view.

Miracles can leave us confused. The Lazarus story is full of drama. Lazarus emerges from the tomb still wearing his burial clothing. 'The dead man came out, his hands and feet swathed in linen bands, his face wrapped in a cloth. Jesus said, "Loose him; and let him go."' John 11.44. The message is that Jesus is 'the resurrection and the life'. This is what Jesus can do for every man. By the time that John was writing, this was the post-Easter testimony … Jesus has power over life and death.

Perhaps we must look at the life of Jesus purely in terms of the Kingdom of God. He certainly lived as though the Kingdom was present. It is like a seed in the ground or the yeast in the dough. It is amongst us. God will reign in the world. This, as we saw, was his direct link with John the Baptist. John looked forward to the Kingdom, Jesus stated that it has already dawned. To help us understand 'the mystery of the Kingdom of God', Jesus teaches with parables. And he reassures John the Baptist with the words, 'The blind receive their sight, and the lame walk, the lepers are cleansed, and the deaf hear.' These are the signs of the Kingdom.

Chapter Seven

DID JESUS GET IT WRONG?

We learn by our mistakes. A child discovers the wonder of walking by falling down! It is not an easy learning task. There are no books or manuals to help you with this walking business. This was certainly my experience in the early months of wearing the dog collar. I had read books … and they proved of little worth. My wife, D'rene, and I were on a steep learning curve. It really was a mountain to climb.

I was lucky. Auntie Esther with her husband, Tom, and the two adopted sons, Will and George, had provided me with the base camp for that testing first year in the Parish of Cwmdare in the valleys of South Wales.

Esther was one of the church wardens and quickly adopted us. Sunday night supper at Esther's was for us the high spot in the week. One evening was exceptional. D'rene and I had thoroughly enjoyed ourselves. Neighbours had popped heads around the door, tales had been coloured, and walls had bulged with laughter as the reminiscences grew in the telling. We set off for home with light steps. All was well in the world.

That was the night that Auntie Esther's Tom in the small hours quietly came down the stairs, disturbing no-one in the household. The next morning, Esther found him hanging in the kitchen. Tom was dead. We could not believe that the tragedy had happened.

We searched our consciences. There had to be a reason. Tom had been so normal that Sunday evening, full of tease and fun. With his slight stammer you could never guess what he would say next. Now it was over.

In a while, we realised that Tom had been deeply disturbed, knowing that he was suffering from serious hardening of the arteries; he had rationalised the implications as unacceptable. His little knowledge of medicine had proved to be dangerous. For many years Tom had been a member of the ambulance team underground and had attended many lectures given by the doctor as part of the training. Sadly, he had not shared with the family his fears for the future. The contrast to this mental state was that wonderful last evening we had shared together. In the midst of the fun and laughter, Tom had already bought the rope that he was to use in his suicide. Even today, I find it difficult to understand.

I have discussed Tom's death with many people and find one inescapable conclusion. We may think that we understand the person in front of us. The truth is that we have no idea of the inner suffering endured by those about us and even less concept of what actually goes on in any person's mind. We must then take this thought further. We are not in the position to offer free advice to anyone; as we can never be absolutely certain that we are hearing the complete truth. Also, we can hardly be in a position to pass judgement as most of us barely understand ourselves.

It was many years later that the Bishop of Liverpool, Clifford Martin, on the eve of his retirement, expressed the same thought to me.

"I hope in my forty-five years in the ministry that I have never given any advice to anyone, but I pray that I was given the wisdom to ask the questions, which they were afraid to ask of themselves."

Jesus was faced with the same problems. He became almost completely caught up with demands of people. Word had gone out far and wide that here was a man who was doing wonders. If half of what they heard about him was true, it was worth while carrying your sick friends to him, packing a bag and setting out in pursuit of him. It was worth a try. And that is exactly what they did. They even tore open the roof of a house and lowered a sick person on his cot to the feet of Jesus.

They pursued Jesus.

I too have been pursuing him and it has not been easy. I suspect that my main problem has been this word 'God'. Think about the word 'God'! What comes into your mind when the word appears? In my case very little!

Yet I am aware of a presence that I cannot explain. I know and feel that God is present in our churches and with his people, but it gets harder to see and realise his presence. We pray to God in church and I find it difficult. Churches are not always entirely helpful and I have spent a lifetime in pew and pulpit. I am more and more puzzled as we pray in church … part of the trouble is that I cannot quite hear what is being said because I am going deaf! Too often there is mumbling by those who lead us in prayer. It is often rather a tiresome list of troubled places … Iran, Afghanistan, most of Africa and so on. We seem to skip through exactly the same shopping list Sunday by Sunday.

'Lord, hear our prayer.'

'Lord, humbly hear us.'

Sometimes that response is changed, but I never quite hear what it is in time to use it.

We fill our thoughts with images, formulae and concepts that trip glibly off our tongue and we all do it. As a young man I was assured that the Free Church was better at prayer than we Anglicans were. This I believed, until in one Methodist Church in South Wales I actually heard the minister include the phrase: 'Dear Father in Heaven, as you would have read in yesterday's Western Mail.' At least, we Anglicans can indulge in the repetition of the same set prayers on most Sundays in the year … this helps a little because at least I know what is coming and do my best to tune in to the theme.

I note that our Moslem friends … and remember that I have worked with them all my life … cannot mention the Holy One's name without adding a repetitious cliché such as 'May his name be praised'. I hasten to add that, in the bigotry of our present climate, I almost hesitated to write that last sentence. This is an example of how we religious folk have to watch our backs. What an odd bunch we all are! No wonder so many people dismiss us 'God botherers', as worthless or, even worse, fanatics and dangerous.

But there can only be one God by definition! That means that all the 'world religions' are dealing with the same problems as we pursue our God. It also suggests that we should never disparage each other, but we should check each other's progress as we obviously need each other whether we like it or not. Sadly, even the different brands of Christianity too often believe that they have the complete answers and that they are 'the way, the truth and the light'. All other Christians are written off. We should be ashamed of ourselves.

I still recall the occasion when I told a lady that I was a Canon of Liverpool Cathedral and her retort was … "you are not a Christian then!" She belonged to an evangelical group with a direct line to God and obviously believed that she and her lot had the complete truth. No wonder we have problems in finding the Way.

Back to prayer. When those leading us in prayer use the phrase 'We now have a moment for silent prayer', it often means that they have turned over two pages by mistake and need a bit of time to organise their thoughts. Simply, I welcome the moments of silence in our churches. Truly silence is golden, which is why Jesus rose early in the morning and went apart to a hillside. Words can get in the way.

How often do we say, 'It is God's will.'? In other words leave it all to God … accept that God is in complete charge of your life. It sounds to me like an opt-out. We are too lazy to think and investigate and blame it all on God. This can be a habit which produces the next phrase: 'Why does God allow that?' How many times have people said to me there cannot be a God because, if he did exist, he would not allow all this misery and sorrow! How can you believe in the existence of such a God? And I reply that neither do I believe in that God. They do not understand. So let's deal with it now.

"Why does God allow that?" was the topmost question when all those little children were killed when the coal tip crushed their school in Aberfan. Blame God. If there is a God, why did he allow this? A moment's thought should have rationalised that it was the stupidity of man which caused Aberfan. We placed all the coal-refuse on a hillside above that school and sited it on a water outlet, which in time turned it into slurry and resulted in the tragedy. The prayer should have been: 'Dear God forgive us for our stupidity!'

I recall being told of a crucifixion by the Japanese of a soldier in the jungle of Burma. The troops were lined up to watch. A voice called out from the ranks, "Where's God in all this?" There was silence until someone called back, "He's up there, mate, suffering like the rest of us."

Why does not God interfere at such times? There is a classical answer to that. God could interfere, but think about it. We are not blocks of wood; we are beings with the ability to think … so we must learn to think. We are not puppets on a string. We are beings who are capable of love … so we must learn how to love. A parent must allow a child to fall in order that the toddler learns how to walk. A parent who wraps a child in cotton wool is failing the child. The mother who coddles her child like a puppeteer pulling strings is doing more harm than good. So, the mother suffers when the child with the abrasion on her knee cries, and then surrounds her child with love. "Kiss it better, mummy!" In this way the child learns how to become an adult, but sadly the pain is part of the learning process. "He's up there, mate, suffering like the rest of us!" If we are to learn, we have to suffer. We should learn from the futility of war! In the end there always has to be a compromise. Yet again and again, we kill in the name of … and I am lost for words. God is not a puppet-master pulling our strings. You cannot force your children to love you, you have to earn their respect and you have to learn how to love each other. Will mankind ever learn to love God and to love our neighbour?

But to whom are we talking when we 'speak to God?' I truly feel that there is a 'being of purpose and reality' about me. Of course, I know that all my thoughts can only be anthropomorphic and that I only have words to describe my thoughts. I mutter about ultimate goodness and ultimate truth and I realise that they are beyond my wildest conception. And as I read that now, it makes little sense. I have little, if any, conception of what the word 'God' means. What God is remains for me completely hidden. I am only encouraged by the occasional Episcopal letter which is equally veiled in mystery, but it assures me of God's blessing. We are rather glib in our use of the word God.

I take heart from John 1. 18: 'No one has ever seen God. It is God the only Son, who is close to the Father's heart, who has made him known.' That is a fascinating sentence. 'No one has ever seen God', but only by knowing Jesus can we know anything about God. This is encouraging because my entire efforts are to discover Jesus. Maybe I know more about God than I realise.

Maybe I am on the right track in this God business … find Jesus and you will find God.

I passed through a period in my life when I was told that science was unravelling all mysteries, but where there are gaps in knowledge, those spaces are filled by God. I was working for 'God in the Gaps'. I assumed those scientists thought that the gaps would be slowly filled and that would be the end of God.

Life is not like that. We all have enquiring minds and should use them. A God who fears progress in human knowledge is not much of a God. Of course, there is so much that is beyond my understanding … and as I read book after book I know it applies to all thinking men. The more we know, the more there is to know. But, the old saying about 'not seeing the wood for the trees' comes to mind. I tend to forget that for many years I actually have known all that I need to know about God. God is love. The trouble is that it seems to be too simple, yet I cannot let that thought go. God is love. I have a good working knowledge about the power of love. Perhaps that is all that I need to know.

'For love is of God, and anyone who loves, is born of God and knows God. Anyone who does not love, does not know God, for God is love.' 1 John 4. 8.

Behavioural science is working to explain 'love' as an extension of the pack caring for its own. That rather amazes me. My vision tells me that at Christmas time when the family tends to collect around the turkey that is the very time when the family 'pack' is at its greatest danger of disintegrating. Going away as a family on holidays can spark off the end of the family! Mankind too often does not thrive very well as a pack … unless, of course, real love is present.

I have actually read the theory that the Trinity is essential to the concept of love because there has to be an object of love before it can exist. Love cannot exist on its own. Happily I seem to have lost that particular book.

This concept of a God of Love also takes a beating when we come to suffering. I find it impossible to advise a lady suffering the agonies of severe arthritis that she should 'sublimate the pain and think of the glory that lies ahead.' I fail to see the will of God in that situation. Even worse, we are told by some Christians that pain is meant to be a test of our faith. And the ultimate nonsense is that pain is a means of doing penance for our sins! All of this I have heard from fellow clergy and it fills me with despair. They are describing a cruel tyrant and not a loving God.

The world is full of pain. Jesus also rebelled against pain and suffering and injustice … it was his natural response to human need.

So far in this chapter I have expressed the thoughts which confuse most of us. Of course there is no confusion if you have closed your mind and accept that it is all God's will. If you think everything is God's will, you are stuck with it. You can do nothing, think nothing and be nothing. You just wait for God to pull the strings and, I suppose, be thankful. That is not the world that I recognise. Our world is in a mess and we are daily adding to the chaos of that mess. This is where we live.

Paul in his letter to the Galatians, chapter 5. 19-21, describes what he saw in the world about him. It reads like any of today's daily newspapers.

'The works of the flesh are obvious: fornication, impurity, licentiousness, idolatry, sorcery, enmities, strife, jealousy, anger, quarrels, dissensions, factions, envy, drunkenness, carousing, and things like these.'

If you are at a loose end, tick off each symptom against the articles in your morning paper. I suspect you will have some difficulty in finding articles about 'love and goodness and fidelity'.

So far I have been writing about the confusion and problems that face all of us. And that was the world that faced Jesus. He met confusion, problems and failure in his ministry in Galilee.

Jesus lived in a world full of pain. His time with John the Baptist had briefed him fully about enmities, strife, anger and dissensions. The renegades north of Galilee were making a lifestyle of fostering dissent and that was where John was at work. He had started his ministry there at the same time as the arrival of the procurator Pontius Pilate as Roman governor and Agrippa Herod, who became Agrippa I, King of the Jews. John was a powerful preacher and knew that there had to be political upheaval. He was in favour of rejecting Rome and hoped that God would intervene to establish a new king and high priest over the world of the Jews. This was the Messiah ... the king above all kings

Josephus writes about John the Baptist: 'When others too joined the crowds about him, because they were aroused to the highest degree by his sermons, Herod became alarmed. Eloquence that had so great an effect on mankind might lead to some kind of sedition (or revolt). For it looked as if they would be guided by John in everything that they did. Herod decided therefore that it would be much better to strike first and be rid of him before his work led to an uprising.'

Before his beheading, John sent some of his disciples to ask Jesus an important question: 'Are you the one who is to come, or are we to wait for another? Are you going to be the one who will bring about the salvation of the Jews?'

The Jews were living in a hard world and were impatient for the 'new kingdom' … this was the message of John the Baptist. 'Thy kingdom come, thy will be done' was a cry from the heart, as Jesus well knew. John equated repentance and baptism as necessary to embrace the Kingdom. To be a 'good Jew' that was the way into the Kingdom. Having baptised Jesus, it seems odd that John remained unsure of his cousin's future role.

Jesus was obviously attracted to the teaching of John the Baptist, but moved on to the idea that the Kingdom is already dawning. It was not the same Kingdom that John had proclaimed. His concept of the Kingdom was new.

As we have stated before the answer to John's question was explicit. 'Go and tell John what you hear and see; the blind receive their sight, the lame walk, the lepers are cleansed, the deaf hear, the dead are raised, and the poor have good news brought to them.' Matthew 11. 4. Incidentally, the poor are those low in spiritual strength … 'poor in spirit'. The 'poor in spirit' are those who desperately need their God and that was the right attitude to secure entry into the Kingdom of God. This was not what John the Baptist wanted to hear.

We are not told how John reacted to this message. Jesus added, 'And blessed is anyone who takes no offence at me.' Sadly that is exactly what happened.

The Pharisees had control of the Synagogues in every town, and tradition ruled all thought. They were the 'religious universities' of the day. The Law was discussed and analysed and there they prayed for the revival of Israel. Changes in tradition were not accepted. Almost from the beginning of his ministry, the Pharisees opposed Jesus. Their complacency and hypocrisy (the word is used fifteen times in Matthew's Gospel) was too much for him and he said so. Jesus did not disregard the Law of Moses which was so dear to the hearts of the Pharisees, but felt that it did not go far enough. 'The law and the prophets were in effect until John came; since then the good news of the Kingdom of God.' Luke 16. 16. Another subtle change was Jesus seemed less concerned with rules, but he seemed to look for obedience from his followers. He frequently used the phrase, 'but I say unto you'. This was revolutionary talk. Very soon the Pharisees were plotting to arrest him and Jesus found himself in a head-on clash with Judaism.

Jesus was being rejected on other grounds. His own townspeople said 'Is not this the carpenter's son? Is not his mother called Mary? Are not his brothers James and Joseph and Simon? Are not all his sisters with us? Where then did this man get all this? And they took offence at him.' Matthew 13. 55. The desertion of his own family … which contradicts the pious birth legends of Matthew and Luke … must have made him feel truly despondent. 'Who are my mother and my brothers? Whoever does the will of God are my brother and sister and mother.' Mark 3. 34.

The mission in Galilee was falling apart. This was reflected in his parables. The Parable of the Sower sowing seed on useless soil … 'who hear the word of God but fail to understand it.' Mark 4. The Parable of the Vineyard talks of the 'stone which the builders rejected'.

Even the miracles were not helping his mission. He had alienated the ordinary people who did not understand his teachings and only saw a 'wonder-man'. Some followers planned to 'seize him and declare him to be king'. That was not his message. They had not understood. He had been repudiated by the leaders of Judaism, the Pharisees and Scribes. He was rejected by his family and was beginning to feel isolated. The Roman overlords were seeing him as a political threat hell-bent on political subversion. Prince Herod Antipas had already executed Jesus' teacher, John the Baptist, and was encouraged to move against Jesus.

Conflict seemed to be inevitable. Whatever he did provoked opposition. Healing on the Sabbath, eating with the wrong people, not observing the laws of purity … in the end, not just the self-righteous Pharisees were against him, they were joined by the chief priests, elders, and scribes. The people, who were complaining were not bad or evil, they did not understand and saw him as a trouble maker.

The two years in Galilee could not be described as a success. His ministry had to be abandoned. It was time for a dramatic U-turn.

We read in Mark 8. 27 onwards: 'Jesus went on with his disciples to the villages of Caesarea Philippi; and on the way he asked his disciples, "Who do people say that I am?" And they answered him, "John the Baptist; and others Elijah; and still others, one of the prophets." He asked them, "But who do you say I am?" Peter answered him, "You are the Messiah". And he sternly ordered them not to tell anyone about him.'

This was the watershed in the Gospels. From this time onwards, Jesus concentrated on his disciples. The atmosphere was to change. Jesus began to talk about the violent end which was coming to him. The disciples had to be prepared for what lay ahead. Jesus now turned his face towards Jerusalem and he must have known that if Galilee had turned against him, Jerusalem would prove to be lethal. His message had been rejected in Galilee so it was essential that he had to take his mission to the centre of the community. He had no desire to die, but he knew that it would be inevitable

Where did the thoughts about death come from? The answer is clear. Many Jews in the time of Jesus were well versed in scripture and its implications for the plight of the Jewish nation. It was studied and discussed in every village synagogue.

At Caesarea Philippi he had firmly told Peter to tell no man that he was the Messiah, because he knew that it would be misunderstood. Even when he was arrested at Jerusalem and brought before the high priest, he refused to answer the question, 'Are you the Messiah?' He said 'the words are yours'. His idea of being a 'king' was different. He was inaugurating a kingdom, but it was a different kingdom to what was expected.

Jesus like all good Jews was steeped in scripture. Of vital interest were chapters 40-66 of the second Book of the Prophet Isaiah. It was probably written about 400 BC and the main theme was the Suffering Servant. There is much mystery about who this servant was … was it the people of Israel or was it an individual to come who would bring God's purpose to fruition. The driving thought was that the Servant would die and bring about God's victory. It was to be victory through suffering. The post-Easter writers very quickly associated the idea to the sufferings of Jesus. They made Jesus the Suffering Servant. It is a natural line of thought and fits perfectly into the Crucifixion and Resurrection. The question that concerns me is whether Jesus saw himself as the Suffering Servant?

Jesus had concluded that he must go to Jerusalem and that he would be put to death by the Jewish hierarchy. It really is possible that he did equate himself with the Suffering Servant who would initiate the new Kingdom. It is well authenticated that he knew what might lie ahead and that he did warn the disciples. One thing is certain … the disciples did not understand the implication of Caesarea Phillipi.

But it happened. The prophet Isaiah had said that he would 'be wounded for our transgressions, and bruised for our iniquities.' God's plan to rescue the world from its evils was set. The Gospels linked his death firmly into the idea of the Suffering Servant. Jesus seemed to have almost rejected the word 'Messiah', but had embraced the Suffering Servant concept. After Caesarea Philippi he dwelt very much on what lay ahead. Second Isaiah's tragic figure was uppermost in his thoughts.

The disciples were incredulous. They were still intent on a world conqueror, and were disappointed.

'Jesus said to his disciples, "What I now say is for you: ponder my words. The Son of Man is going to be given up into the power of men." But they did not understand what he said; it had been hidden from them so that they should not perceive its drift; and they were afraid to ask him what it meant.

A dispute arose among them: which of them was the greatest? Jesus knew what was passing in their minds, so he took a child by the hand and stood him at his side, and said, "Whoever receives this child in my name receives me; and whoever receives me receives the One who sent me. For the least among you all … he is the greatest."'

Luke 9. 43-48.

'Who should be the greatest?' They were still thinking of the earthly kingdom and the possibility of power.

'From that time Jesus began to make it clear to his disciples that he had to go to Jerusalem, and there to suffer much from the elders, chief priests, and lawyers; to be put to death and to be raised again on the third day. At this Peter took him by the arm and began to rebuke him: "Heaven forbid!" he said. "No, Lord, this shall never happen to you." Then Jesus turned and said to Peter, "Away with you, Satan; you are a stumbling-block to me. You think as men think, not as God thinks."'

Matthew 16. 20-23.

The criticism of Peter was totally fierce. It was the way that he had dealt with the temptation by the Devil in the desert when he was offered power over the world. "Get away. Get thee behind me!" Peter the first of the disciples, the leading apostle, had completely failed to grasp the intentions of Jesus.

If his ministry in Galilee had fallen apart as a failure, it now seemed that the future was bleak indeed. There would be little evidence that the disciples ever did grasp his purpose until after the crucifixion. Most of his supporters had long gone and his disciples were little better. When the end came, his disciples, who had been with him for some three years, went into hiding; they ran away, and it was left to someone else to bury him.

In Luke 24. 21 we read of the despair amongst his followers. After the crucifixion, Cleopas, walking on the road to Emmaus expressed the depression of the disciples. "We had been hoping that he was the man to liberate Israel."

What lay ahead was daunting. Yet the miracle happened. His death and resurrection were to become the central point of the spiritual life of millions. In a strange way the failure in Galilee was to lead to ultimate success. It did require a miracle!

Chapter Eight

THE TEACHER

My arrival at Llandaff Cathedral opened up a new world for me ... I had never preached in a Cathedral before and I was rather nervous. But there was to be an even bigger challenge.

My predecessor and old friend, Edwin Davies, had conducted a Children's Service in the Lady Chapel for almost a decade with great success. Edwin had the reputation of being 'good with children'. That Service was to be my responsibility with one major difference. It was to be held in the new nave and not in the small Lady Chapel. The nave was very big and the pulpit so high that you needed oxygen.

My Service was scheduled to last for half an hour, squeezed in between the Parish Eucharist and Cathedral Matins. The numbers attending the Eucharist had rocketed in the newly launched Cathedral and invariably the Service over-ran its time-slot. My vocal congregation of youngsters gathered at the West door, raising the decibel level, as ten o'clock struck and went. At least, they did not sing, 'Why are we waiting'! Then came the charge! As one congregation fought to get out, my tiddlers ferreted their way through them, rushing in to grab the front seats. The Cathedral organist was stopped in full voluntary to be replaced by Marjorie Gibbons, who hit the keys as quickly as possible to deaden the sound. With luck, I could start the

Service by ten past ten; our deadline was ten-forty as we had to evacuate our lot to make way for Cathedral Matins, which was regarded as the holiest of productions in the Cathedral life. Timing was vital.

My little darlings were there, not to raise the tone of the place, but to enjoy an act of worship. You cannot praise God with a miserable face! As we did our stuff, I was aware of the Cathedral Choir rehearsing in the basement of the Prebendal House, adding in our rare moments of silence a sense of the numinous, which I believed was not lost on those young people in the congregation. It was all part of the Cathedral atmosphere.

The format of my service was the proverbial 'hymn sandwich' ... three hymns with chat in between. The chat was the problem. The first slot had to be a Jesus story to stress the impact that He made upon all those about Him. There were plenty of books with ideas and themes. This was to establish a basis of Christian teaching and was not to be a difficulty. The second slot was intended to make the teaching personal and understandable to the vast cross section of ages in front of me. Three-year olds and twelve-year olds are chalk and cheese, but as I gazed down from the pulpit, I realised that they produced another problem, because almost every child had been brought to the Cathedral by his father. Here was a congregation of men and children. The answer was to be Charlie!

Just five weeks into the problem, I told a simple story about a mouse. On the spur of the moment, I called him Charlie. The name proved to be a winner.

Charlie thought that he was a very important mouse,

the most importantest mouse in the mousey world. He knew it was true because he could prove it. After all, he had jumped the highest mountain that any mouse had ever jumped. It was the hugest of jumps.

Using the microphone, I had the children pretend that they were jumping, as up and up we went and then back into our seats with a 'plonk'. Chaos reigned, but it was controlled. Everyone was smiling. Even the dads had joined in the fun!

When Charlie looked back on the mountain, he realised that it had not been much of a mountain. In fact, it was just a clump of grass. Ah well!

Then Charlie came to a large lake, as big as an ocean. You could barely see the other side. Charlie took off and leapt and leapt the biggest leap that had ever been leapt and, with a 'kerplonk', he landed on the other side. Fantastic!!! Yet when he looked back, all that it had been, if you really looked, was a puddle of murky, mucky, dirty water. His tail went down. His whiskers sank. "I'm not much of a mouse!"

Charlie made his way sadly homewards, waggleless and wobbleless, muttering as he went, "Best place is home". Into the barn he crept, where the farmer had conveniently stacked a huge mound of wheat. Charlie felt a little better, because all mouses are rather fond of wheat and this pile of goodies was enough for breakfast for ever and ever and longer than that. So he sat, twiddled his whiskers and thought and scratched, as he thought, and came up with a wonderful conclusion of a thought. "To prove that I'm the greatest mouse that ever was, I'll move this mountain of breakfast from this side of the barn to that side of the barn and that will be the finest thing that I have ever done."

He took one piece of grain, sniffed it, and toddled across the barn. He did it again and again. He began to shout, "I can do it, I can do it." Then he jumped in the air, landed upside down, waggled his feet, gyrated his tail and announced to the world, "I can do it! What a clever mouse I am, I am!"

Charlie stopped and began to think in straight lines. Of course, he could do it, but it would take a long bit of time, many months of bits of time, too many bits of time for a mouse. Charlie thought a while longer and then said in his loudest voice, which filled the barn with all his sound, "I know I can do it, but I'll be the tiredest of mouses." And the more that he thought about that, the tireder he became and, in no time at all, Charlie was fast asleep. Every person in the Cathedral made snoring noises with full crescendos, such as had never been heard in all the centuries of worship in that place.

The last two minutes of the address drove the message home. There are many hills and mountains to be conquered in our lives. Faith might be able to move mountains, but pain and suffering and ache would not go away. Jesus, like Charlie, knew that we can only tackle today what we can manage today. You must do today exactly what you can achieve today. I began to refer thereafter to the 'sacrament of the present moment'. If you do nothing, the mountain can get bigger.

That was the first story about Charlie the Mouse. Next week, I tried a different tale about a pussy cat up to London to see the Queen.

I only became aware of the impact of Charlie the Mouse when a small child dragged her father up to me at the end of that Service and, with all the wonder of toddledom, posed a question.

"Was it Charlie the Mouse that the cat saw under the Queen's chair?" With no hesitation, I replied, "Come next week and we'll have a peep together."

That father looked at me with half a smile.

"See you next week, Bob."

That was when I realised that a child had remembered the Charlie story and was interested in a character, which I should not abandon. Charlie had to be resurrected!

For almost four and half years I stayed with Charlie. Inadvertently, I had found a way into the lives of those toddlers. Charlie was a winner.

Jesus now faced a similar problem. There had to be a 'way in' after the failure of the Galilean ministry.

After Caesarea Philippi Jesus changed tactics. Now he tried to avoid the crowds … after all it had been a disaster. He turned to his disciples. A theme in his teaching was that people are blind even though they have sight and that about summed up his disciples. They were a problem. 'Can the blind lead the blind? Will not they both fall in the pit?' The disciples needed help for what lay ahead. Galilee was over.

The time was right. Remember what had happened at Caesarea Philippi. Mark 8. 27-30. Matthew 16. 13-16. Luke 9. 18-20.

Jesus asks his disciples, "Who do people say that I am?"

"Some say he is John the Baptist; and still others, one of the prophets."
Then Jesus asks, "But who do you say that I am?"

Mark. Peter answered him, "You are the Messiah."

Matthew. Simon Peter answered, "You are the Messiah, the Son of the living God."

Luke. "The Messiah of God."

Perhaps the time in Galilee had not been wasted, but whether the disciples really understood the implication of their answers is a matter of doubt.

There had been much talk about the coming of a Kingdom and the disciples must have discussed it amongst themselves … who will be the leaders in it … and what sort of Kingdom. It had been a busy time … synagogues, Capernaum, the Sea of Galilee and crowds of people. Most of his teaching was aimed at ordinary folk who lived in Galilee. Jesus had healed the sick, the blind, the deaf and those possessed with demons. There had been endless arguments about meals and fasting, the Sabbath and his right to exercise his gifts and power. And in spite of it all, at last Peter voiced what must have been the conclusion of the disciples. Jesus had not put words into their mouths. "You are the Messiah" came from the hearts of the disciples. This was the 'good news', this was the Gospel. The devotional worship of Christ was to come much later, but here was the beginning of the post-Easter adulation.

The reaction of Jesus to Peter's affirmation was dramatic. "Tell no-one." Mark 8. 30. The miracles had caused enough trouble and this outburst from Peter would have been catastrophic … and in fact it was. 'What manner of man is this?' This was not really to be answered until after the death of Jesus. Jesus was intent on keeping his feet on the ground. It was as if he was saying … here I am, I am a man like you, this is where we live; we are in this together. We have a path to tread and it is not going to be easy. Walk with me.

Jesus did not want to talk about himself, but about the Kingdom. This was the centre of his message and it was vital for the disciples to grasp the meaning. It was no airy-fairy concept. 'Thy Kingdom come on earth' was well remembered by those disciples. Keep your feet on the ground. It was all about people, ordinary people … it was 'good news' for the poor in spirit and includes all of us. We all belong to families, now you belong to a Kingdom.

And that, too, could have been misunderstood. Herod and Rome were about kingdoms and the majority of folk would have hoped that this talk about Kingdom was to do with politics and power.

The Kingdom of God was God's intention for the earth. This was the punch line. It was what all life is about. This was a dramatic message for mankind. We are meant to transform the world. This was revolutionary. If they wanted a king, Jesus was announcing a completely new idea for the Kingdom. He was inviting us to become Kingdom people. Let God be your king. Abandon your ideas about freedom from Rome and all your political dreams of nationalism. This Kingdom was for all mankind. And this message did not go down well with his fellow Jews who were versed in the concept of the God of Israel.

How dare this upstart even suggest that the new Kingdom was to embrace the whole world?

Jesus knew that a 'holy war' against Rome was doomed to end in total disaster. The turning point in the history of the nation was very close and did happen. The Temple was to be destroyed irretrievably in the disasters of AD 70 and AD 135. Jesus almost did the same. He was to throw the money changers out of the Temple and charge them with desecration. He wanted an end to a sacrificial system which had dominated the purpose of the building. God was not to be contained in a building. This was revolutionary thinking. It was as though Jesus was destroying the Temple.

Mark 12. 32-34 is important. 'Then the scribe said to him, "You are right, Teacher; you have truly said that 'he is the one, and beside him there is no other' and 'to love him with all your heart, and with all understanding, and with all strength' and 'to love your neighbour as oneself' … this is much more important than all whole burnt offerings and sacrifices". When Jesus saw that he had answered wisely, he said to him, 'You are not far from the Kingdom of God. After that no one dared to ask him any question.'

Jesus was smashing Israel's past and proclaiming a new world where God was supreme. It was much more than a simple moral code. It was a statement that we ordinary people are part of this Kingdom. For the Pharisees and the practising Jew this was all too much. This Jesus was not only proclaiming a new idea of the Kingdom, but seemed to expect people to follow him. No wonder his message was to result in apparent failure on the cross.

Much thought and scholarship has gone into answering the question … did Jesus really see himself as the Messiah? The traditional answer is that Jesus thought that he was the Messiah. Perhaps it does not matter as the evidence is inconclusive. What really matters is that we see him as our King … our Messiah. As we have seen, just once only in Mark at Caesarea Philippi is the question asked and Peter stated clearly 'You are the Messiah … you are our King!' Jesus does not approve or disprove, he merely asks firmly that it should not be discussed. Matthew absorbing Mark's gospel adds you are 'the Son of the living God'. Matthew in the same way adds to the story of the stilling of the storm … 'Truly you are the Son of God'. This surely is the opinion of the post-Easter church. In fact it was that first Christian community after Easter at work. Jesus seemed to have more important matters to communicate to his followers. He does not wish to discuss whether he is King or not.

We need to look at Jesus again. So far we have garnered a few facts only about Jesus before Easter. He had parents, Joseph and Mary and a number of siblings. Joseph was a carpenter and probably Jesus also had that trade. He was from a basic peasant background in a small village in Galilee. He obviously was religious and went to meet John the Baptist to discover what his life was about. The fantastic achievement was that from this background he became in three hundred years the central figure in a religion which dominated the western world. We truly know so little about his pre-Easter life and thoughts.

He certainly was different … he had a mystical aura about him which made people follow him. He was a man of

God and defies our use of words to describe him. He was a man of spirit who had 'Godness' about him. But he was a Jew and his mind was certainly shaped in the synagogues where he became versed in the Jewish scripture.

But what did he think he was doing? There were stories about his ability to heal and cast out demons. Inexplicable things happened. It is not enough to explain his healing as psychosomatic. Whatever happened, the blind were given sight and all manner of sickness was cured. He saw the dangers of these gifts and tried to play them down … his compassion forced him to help those in need, but again and again he asked that his gifts should not be talked about. They were not his primary concern. He did not want to be known as a miracle worker.

This man knew God and that was the driving force of his mission. I believe that he wanted each one of us to know God as he knew him. He was a messenger from God to invite us into the Kingdom of God. His message was from God and he never wavered from his desire for each one of us to share his knowledge of God.

As I write, I realise that I have been steeped in the Christology of the post-Easter Jesus … this is the Jesus of the Christian Creeds. It inevitably colours my thinking. But now I am searching for the historical Jesus. That excites me, but the one does not exclude the other. I live now with the pre-Easter and the post-Easter Christ.

Yet every ounce of my being wants to meet the pre-Easter Jesus. That Jesus was perfect seems to be a pre-requisite of the Gospel. True or false? He certainly ticked off the scribes and Pharisees with a fierceness which seems to lack charity and understanding. He was equally tough on some of the inhabitants of Galilee. Matthew 11. 20-24 is rather explicit … 'I tell you that on the day of judgement it will be more tolerable for the land of Sodom than for you.' There is no sign of the traditional 'Gentle Jesus, meek and mild'. His attitude towards ordinary people could be brutally rude. Mark 7. 24-30 and Matthew 15. 21-28. A Gentile woman asked Jesus to heal her daughter and was at first rejected. He was also rather rough with his own family. To his mother at the wedding in Cana … 'Woman, what have I to do with you?' Mark 3. 31-35. 'Who are my mother and brothers?' And looking around on those who sat about him, he said, 'Here are my mother and my brother! Whoever does the will of God is my brother, and sister and mother.' Mark 10. 17-22. 'Why do you call me good? No-one is good but God alone.' But by the time we come to John's Gospel, it has all toned down and the moral perfection of Jesus is asserted.

Let us take these thoughts further. Did Jesus see himself as God made man? John 8. 58 is fascinating. 'Jesus said to them, "Very truly I tell you before Abraham was, I am." So they picked up stones to throw at him.' The title 'Yahweh', used by the Jews for God's title, and means 'I am'. It is possible that John has gilded the lily with post-Easter thought. We have the same problem with the phrase 'Son of Man'. 'The Son of Man has authority on earth to forgive sins.' It probably means no more than saying that God has delegated this power to me. The first three gospels in no way see the phrase as indicating supernatural power. Maybe we cannot answer the question,

'Did Jesus see himself as God?' It did not seem to be important to Jesus. Scholars have a field day with all the conflicting texts and the books are legion.

Perhaps there is a better starting point in our attempt to find the 'real' Jesus. Let's go back to the concept of the Kingdom of God. Israel would not let go the thought that God would interfere in their history … to their good. They wanted a story that would vindicate them … the Temple, the Law and their freedom was paramount. Jesus knew all this. The people expected it all to happen with a big bang! And here was Jesus wandering around talking about a Kingdom. Was this the Kingdom they longed for? At last was it all about to happen?

The early church adopted almost the same language, but with a subtle twist. They too seemed to expect a 'big bang' and the birth of this Kingdom. But slowly they realised that the Kingdom had already arrived. The technical theological term is 'realised eschatology'. This big bang … the end … had already dawned. No orthodox Jew could possibly accept that. So it came about that the early Christians were abandoning the Jewish hope of their Kingdom. This was a new concept of a Kingdom. God's Kingdom was for the whole world, for all people, and it was established by Jesus of Nazareth. This was a vital message that Jesus had conveyed to those early disciples; they could not have created that thought.

At the start of his ministry Jesus said: 'Repent! For the Kingdom of heaven is at hand.' That was Mark. Writing a little later, Matthew emphasises that Jesus came for the purpose of 'preaching the Gospel of the Kingdom.' Many of the parables had the Kingdom theme, none more than the Parable of the Sower. There are three versions of it. It is telling the story of Israel … they are part of the thorns and the stones and the failure of the seed. The seed is God's word strangled and killed by the unyielding ground. There is then the good news … the gospel … the rocks and thorns are over and no longer important. The story is really about Jesus. He has sown the good seed in good ground and the harvest is now. Jesus said, 'If you have ears to hear, then hear!' The Jews found it offensive. This is a Kingdom story, a wake-up story. 'The Kingdom of God is at hand'. Jesus says you have to believe it. 'Repent and believe the Gospel'.

Read the parables as kingdom stories and it all makes sense. This leads me on to consider the meaning of the Kingdom of God for me. From childhood I have absorbed the Sermon on the Mount and the Lord's Prayer … the latter in the old version because it is deep in my thoughts.

Let's start with the Sermon on the Mount. It must be obvious that the evangelists are responsible for the format of the Sermon. Scholars are well divided about the way in which the early church assembled the sayings, but most agree that these were true Jesus-thoughts. They are not just moral statements, but almost a game plan for the new Kingdom … the new law for Kingdom-seekers.

'Blessed are the poor in spirit, for theirs is the Kingdom of heaven.
Blessed are those who mourn, for they will be comforted.

Blessed are the meek, for they will inherit the earth.
Blessed are those who hunger and thirst for righteousness, for they will be filled.
Blessed are the merciful, for they will receive mercy.
Blessed are the pure in heart, for they will see God.
Blessed are the peacemakers, for they will be called children of God.
Blessed are those who are persecuted for righteousness' sake, for theirs is the kingdom of heaven.'

This was a message for each one of us. It is the agenda for those who would follow Jesus into his Kingdom. When I reflect upon my life, I realise that it all makes sense because God has been with me every step of the way, whether I was aware or not of his presence. This Sermon is much more than a moral code, it is a promise that Jesus is with me at all times. This is life in the Kingdom of God and it is for each one of us.

Now turn to the Lord's Prayer. What the original form of this prayer was cannot be determined and matters not. We have the words which were used in the early church. If the disciples asked Jesus to teach them how to pray, the early church has put the thoughts in an orderly form for each one of us. This is how we pray. This is the prayer for those in the Kingdom of heaven. Here is Matthew's version.

'Pray then this way:

Our Father in heaven,
hallowed be your name.
Your Kingdom come.

Your will be done,
on earth as it is in heaven.
Give us this day our daily bread.
And forgive us our debts,
as we also have forgiven our debtors
And do not bring us to the time of temptation,
but rescue us from the evil.'

Other manuscripts add:

'For the kingdom and the power and the glory
are yours for ever.
Amen.'

Matthew 6. 9-11.

This prayer gives us a shape and a form of prayer. However, it clearly is a prayer meant for those of the Kingdom of God. Like many Christians I have used it frequently as a meditation. It is part of the Kingdom agenda and firmly part of me.

This Kingdom is not really about heaven, it is about me here on earth. 'Your Kingdom come on earth' is a clear statement. A place where there is enough to eat, a place of justice and of peace. This is God's Kingdom. This is God's promise for the future of mankind. The Beatitudes and the Lord's Prayer spell out the good news of the Gospel. This is God's dream for the world.

In this Kingdom there is to be total forgiveness. We accept each other as fellow members of this Kingdom. Our main enemy is evil; that is the cancer to be eradicated and it affects each one of us … we need the help of God to deal with it.

The thoughts are basic and face us all with a challenge. We are part of the struggle. We are called to be part of this kingdom.

There was much talk about 'final judgement' and 'end of the world'. I am not sure that the end of the world means just that. I think that it means the end of the world as we know it. It is not the end of the physical world, not the disappearance of the earth, but the disappearance of the old world, rather the transformation of the old world. There is much debate about this … so many books … and you take your pick!

Was the end to happen almost immediately?

Was God going to interfere any time in his time?

Would it be very clear to all that it had happened?

There is plenty of evidence in the New Testament that the end of the world and the final judgement were thought to be imminent. 'Truly I tell you, this generation will not pass away until all these things have taken place.' Mark 11. 30.

But it did not happen. Was Jesus totally deluded and confused? Again you take your pick with scholars. Let's try to make it simple.

Albert Schweitzer, who probably started the modern search for the historical Jesus, wrote some very famous words that bear reading again and again. Here they are.

'He comes to us as one Unknown, without a name, as of old, by the lakeside, He came to those men who knew Him not. He speaks to us the same word: "Follow thou me! and sets us to the tasks which he has to fulfil for our time. He commands. And to those who obey Him, whether they be wise or simple, He will reveal Himself in the toils, the conflicts, the sufferings which they shall pass through in His fellowship, and as an ineffable mystery, they shall learn in their own experience Who He is.'

This is the Christ who still speaks to us. His message is that we follow him and for us that means now. We are meant to walk with God in his Kingdom now with all our toils and conflicts and sufferings. St. Augustine put it into far better language. 'God without us will not; and we without God cannot.'

The bottom line for the Kingdom people had been made very clear. Love God and love your neighbour. That is the purpose of your life. If you think about it, it is the hardest thing to do. On your own you will fail. We cannot do it without God. We need the second coming of Jesus in our own lives.

Go back two thousand years. Perhaps we should not be surprised that the disciples did not understand. Of course they were confused and puzzled even though they had travelled with Jesus! Others followed for equally mixed up reasons. Surely those whom he healed would attempt to follow. Surely those wishing to be healed would follow with hope. It all seemed to be rather futile. In the end Jesus had to take the entire burden on is own shoulders. They did not understand.

There was to be only one way to convince us that we are to be part of God's Kingdom. Only Jesus could establish the Kingdom and it would cost him his life.

Chapter Nine

HE DIED FOR ME

Maybe it was just a dream. Imagine it. The world at peace. Mankind at ease with itself. Man at one with God. No more blindness. No more hate. No more misunderstanding. Freedom from bondage. The world of Jesus was not like that. It was no dream world … but harsh and cruel.

For thirty years the Jews had been under the heel of Rome. The Temple authorities ruled under the control of a High Priest who had been appointed by Rome. Those with wealth called all the shots. That's the way it was.

The potential for violence boiled beneath the surface of society. And Jesus was involved. His endless talk of the Kingdom of God seemed to be no more than a form of non-violent resistance and his sniping at authority was to lead to his death. To many he was just a rabble-rouser.

The events of his last week of life seemed inevitable. That final Passover festival in Jerusalem was like dry tinder waiting for the flame. Jerusalem was the focus of all attention. It was the centre of political control and the Passover was the potential flame.

The Passover was a vital festival celebrating the exodus from Egypt … the beginning of the nation … and it exuded the word 'liberation'. Rome had always expected trouble at the Passover as thousands assembled for the Feast. The Imperial

Guard was strengthened alongside the Temple. They were ready for it.

The Gospels recall the events on a daily basis. Mark devotes the majority of his thoughts to that last week and Matthew copies them almost word for word.

Here at last we may have a chance to sight the true Jesus, the historical Jesus who has proved so elusive in our journey.

The Sunday

Mark 11. 1-11.

'They were now approaching Jerusalem, and when they reached Bethphage and Bethany, at the Mount of Olives, he sent two of his disciples with these instructions: 'Go to the village opposite, and, just as you enter, you will find tethered there a colt which no one has yet ridden. Untie it and bring it here. If anyone asks, "Why are you doing that?" say, "Our Master needs it, and will send it back here without delay." So they went off, and found the colt tethered to a door outside in the street. They were untying it when some of the bystanders asked, "What are you doing, untying that colt?" They answered as Jesus had told them, and were then allowed to take it. So they brought the colt to Jesus and spread their cloaks on it, and he mounted. And people carpeted the road with their cloaks, while others spread brushwood which they had cut in the fields; and those who went ahead and the others who came behind shouted, "Hosanna! Blessings on him who comes in the name of the Lord! Blessings on the coming kingdom of our father David! Hosanna in the heavens!" He entered Jerusalem and went into the temple, where he looked at the whole scene; but, as it was now late, he went out to Bethany with the Twelve.'

It was a tough journey from Jericho, the lowest city on Earth, some eight hundred feet below sea level, in a matter of a dozen miles or so to Jerusalem, three thousand feet above sea level. When after travelling through the dry empty land you suddenly arrived, Jerusalem was a vision of luxuriant growth, wonder and wealth. For the Jew this was the chosen place where God had centred himself and given hope for the future. The Passover was a time of prayer and dancing, singing and feasting. This was dream time. If there was to be a Kingdom … now was the time.

Jesus seems to have entered into the swing of things. He processed into the city in style. What a welcome he received! We put cloaks on the ground to receive royalty. Mark makes it quite clear that Jesus entered Jerusalem as a King. This was a moment of triumph. Welcome to the Kingdom of David. The entire episode must have been planned. It was deliberate. The event was based on the prophet Zechariah that a King would enter Jerusalem on the colt of a donkey. He would be a King of peace; this was the Kingdom of their dreams. Zechariah 9. 8-10.

He rode into the city at the same time as the Roman governor, Pontius Pilate, arrived. Pilate came through a different gate. Good timing! It was a blatant political demonstration. The Kingdom of God versus the Kingdom of imperial Rome.

We now call it Palm Sunday and on that day the gauntlet had been thrown down.

The Monday

Mark 11. 15-17.

'So they came to Jerusalem, and he went into the temple and began driving out those who bought and sold in the temple. He upset the tables of the money-changers and the seats of the dealers in pigeons; and he would not allow anyone to use the temple court as a thoroughfare for carrying goods. Then he began to teach them, and said, "Does not scripture say, 'My house shall be called a house of prayer for all the nations'? But you have made it a robber's cave.'

The Temple was not doing its job, not fulfilling its purpose, and was as useless as a barren fig tree. The fig tree symbolised the Temple. The tree withered and died. Was that the future for the Temple?

It got worse. Jesus created mayhem in the Temple. It was the equivalent of entering the House of Commons by force and throwing out the mace. Jesus saw the Temple as no longer acceptable. The sacrificial system depended upon money-changing and animal purchase. Jesus put a stop to it. He was not condemning commercialism, but the whole system of Judaism. It was not part of his Kingdom. Everything that you ask for in prayer will be given you! This was the new Kingdom.

Out with the old. The whole crowd would have approved of his action, even though they probably had no concept of his motives. It is always good to see those who rule being brought down to earth. The hierarchy did nothing because they were afraid, but it did not mean that no action would be taken.

Round One had been against imperial power. Round Two was against the Jewish authority. There could only be one outcome.

The Tuesday and the Wednesday

There followed two days of confrontation and Mark devoted much space to it. At the end of that time Jesus had turned all the Jewish authorities against him, the Pharisees, the Herodians and the Sadducees.

Jesus marches again into the Temple and the crowds watch and listen. He has his gallery and it was a day-out for the mob. They try to trap Jesus.

Mark 11. 27-33

'They came once more to Jerusalem. And as he was walking in the temple court the chief priests, lawyers, and elders came to him and said, "By what authority are you acting like this? Who gave you authority to act in this way?" Jesus said to them, "I will ask you one question; and if you give me an answer, I will tell you by what authority I act. The baptism of John: was it from God, or from men? Answer me." This set them arguing among themselves: "What shall we say? If we say, "From God", he will say, "Then why did you not believe him?" Shall we say, "From men"? But they were afraid of the people, for all held that John was in fact a prophet. So they answered Jesus, "We do not know." and Jesus said to them, "Then neither will I tell you by what authority I act."'

The authority of Jesus is called to account. 'By what right are you doing these things?' Who does this young man think he is! And Jesus goes straight into attack. He questions their authority and the chief priests, the scribes and elders end up looking foolish.

Jesus certainly had entered the city as a King, but he made no reference to it. You might remember that John the Baptist had asked the same question. 'Who are you?' 'What are you?' The answer would by the end of the week be given to that straight question. "Are you the Messiah?" "I am" replied Jesus and that answer ensured the death sentence. 'I am' was the Jewish pseudo-name for God.

But on that Tuesday the verbal battle continued and Jesus used a parable.

Mark 12. 1-12.

'He went on to speak to them in parables: "A man planted a vine yard and put a wall round it, hewed out a winepress, and built a watchtower; then he let it out to vine-growers and went abroad. When the vintage season came, he sent a servant to the tenants to collect from them his share of the produce. But they took him, thrashed him, and sent him away empty-handed. Again, he sent them another servant, whom they beat about the head and treated outrageously. So he sent another, and that one they killed; and many more besides, of whom they beat some, and killed others. He had now only one left to send, his own dear son. In the end he sent him. "They will respect my son", he said. But the tenants said to one another, "This is the heir; come, let us kill him, and the property will be ours." So they seized him and killed him, and flung his body out of the vineyard. What will the owner of the vineyard do? He will come and put the tenants to death and give the vineyard to others. "Can it be that you have never read this text: 'The stone which the builders rejected has become the main cornerstone? This is the Lord's doing, and it is wonderful in our eyes?" Then they began to look for a way to arrest him, for they saw that the parable was aimed at them; but they were afraid of popular feeling, so they left him alone and went away.'

The vineyard is Israel and the greedy tenants are the wealthy and powerful people who are exploiting the situation. It was an obvious attack on the authority of the temple. It had been a stark warning. This parable was an indictment of the heart of Judaism and it could end in only one way. Jesus almost says 'I am the stone that is missing, the capstone, the stone that completes this building.'

The verbal battle continued with a well-known saying, 'Render unto Caesar the things that are Caesar's, and to God the things that are God's.'

Mark 12. 13-17.

'A number of Pharisees and men of Herod's party were sent to trap him with a question. They came and said, "Master, you are an honest man, we know, and truckle to no man, whoever he may be; you teach in all honesty the way of life that God requires. Are we or are we not permitted to pay taxes to the Roman Emperor? Shall we pay or not?" He saw how crafty their question was, and said, "Why are you trying to catch me out? Fetch me a silver piece, and let me look at it." They brought one, and he said to them, "Whose head is this, and whose inscription?" "Caesar's", they replied. Then Jesus said, "Pay Caesar what is due to Caesar, and pay God what is due to God." And they heard him with astonishment.'

The Jews were burdened with taxes. Rome made its demands, Galilee had its cut, the Temple did not miss a trick and even Herod expected his dues. Taxes were not popular, but the trap was not about taxes. It was an attempt to get Jesus to incite rebellion against Rome and that would have been a capital charge.

Jesus' reply was brilliant. The Pharisees had no response. Their plan to get Jesus arrested had failed.

Later that day Judas made a move which hastened the end. He set out to betray Jesus. We cannot but ask why he did it. Mark gives no reason. The other Gospels imply that the motive was money and that Satan drove him to it. Both statements are rather thin.

A further look is required. Judas was trusted by Jesus and acted as treasurer for the twelve, which does suggest that money was hardly a motive to betray a person you have lived alongside for almost three years. Look again. Judas was unlike the other disciples because he came from a different region of Israel. He was Yorkshire and they were all Lancashire. He was North Wales and they were South Wales. Possibly his expectations were different. He might have misunderstood all this Kingdom talk. This man Jesus could be a real King, he could lead a rising against Rome, but it was not happening. Is it possible that Judas thought he could force Jesus to take action in order to avoid being arrested? Surely Jesus would not allow himself to be taken by the authorities. That could be a good and logical reason to 'betray' Jesus. Force Jesus to show his hand. A political motive makes sense.

We have fairly recently discovered the 'Gospel of Judas' … a document written in the second century. In this document Jesus actually tells Judas to betray him! This is behind the speculation that Jesus planned his own death. But scholars have discounted this document as of no historical value concerning the life of Jesus.

I prefer the thought that Judas was growing disgruntled about the way that the Kingdom proposition was taking a wrong turn. Judas was not a bad man, but a misguided man. But your guess is as good as mine.

The future was now inevitable. As far as the Jewish authority was concerned, Jesus was playing politics. His talk of the Kingdom would upset the status quo. The Temple was threatened by him and the security and standing of the priests were also challenged.

Jesus had entered Jerusalem as a King.

Jesus had threatened the financial basis of the Temple.

One of his followers had even anointed Jesus. Kings are anointed.

'Jesus was at Bethany, in the house of Simon the leper. As he sat at table, a woman came in carrying a small bottle of very costly perfume, oil of pure nard. She broke it and poured the oil over his head.'

Mark 14. 3

The High Priest would challenge him, 'Are you the Messiah?' The Roman governor would taunt him with the words, 'This is

Jesus, the King of the Jews.'

All that was left for Jesus to do was to prepare his disciples for what was about to happen. That would be difficult.

The Thursday

'Now on the first day of Unleavened Bread, when the Passover lambs were being slaughtered, his disciples said to him, "Where would you like us to go and prepare for your Passover supper?" So he sent out two of his disciples with these instructions: "Go into the city, and a man will meet you carrying a jar of water. Follow him, and when he enters a house give this message to the householder: "The Master says, 'Where is the room reserved for me to eat the Passover with my disciples?" He will show you a large room upstairs, set out in readiness. Make the preparations for us there." Then the disciples went off, and when they came into the city they found everything just as he had told them. So they prepared for Passover.

In the evening he came to the house with the Twelve. As they sat at supper Jesus said, "I tell you this: one of you will betray me … one who is eating with me." At this they were dismayed; and one by one they said to him, "Not I, surely?" "It is one of the Twelve", he said, "who is dipping into the same bowl with me. The Son of Man is going the way appointed for him in the scriptures; but alas for that man by whom the Son of Man is betrayed! It would be better for that man if he had never been born."

During supper he took bread, and having said the blessing he broke it and gave it to them, with the words: "Take this; this is my body." Then he took a cup, and having offered thanks to God he gave it to them; and they all drank from it. And he said, "This is my blood of the covenant, shed for many. I tell you this: never again shall I drink from the fruit of the vine until that day when I drink it new in the Kingdom of God."'

Mark 14. 12-25

I have made my communion in many places … on the bonnet of a lorry, in an aircraft-hangar; on the chart table of a ship, at many a bedside, in umpteen cathedrals and churches, bishops galore and nobodies-in-particular. On most occasions I felt the presence of Jesus alongside. It works for me.

For many Christians it is a matter of bitter dispute, tiresome argument and serious splits in so-called Christian bodies. We cannot even agree on the title … Last Supper, the Mass, the Eucharist, Holy Communion … and the churches are divided.

This is sad and, at my time of life, rather missing the point. We have a desperate need to remove the ecclesiastical baggage and look again at the Maundy Thursday. Jesus certainly intended it to be central in the thoughts of his disciples.

Incidentally, it is included in the first three Gospels, but not in John. And, of course, we find it in I Corinthians 11. 13-17. In John's Gospel, Jesus got up, took off his robe and washed his disciples' feet. There then follows a long discourse, but let us concentrate on the evening meal that Jesus shared with the disciples.

We cannot even agree as to whether it was a Passover meal or not. It certainly had the semblance of it. Remember that the Passover was celebrated in memory of the deliverance from Egypt … the Exodus. It certainly looked forward to the freedom of Israel and the concept that God was the King. That is a Passover thought and it tuned into Christ's thoughts about Kingdom.

Was Jesus seeing the meal as the new exodus … the Temple is finished and the new Kingdom is at hand? He certainly identified the bread with his own body and the wine with his own blood. He stresses that it is the last meal before the coming of the Kingdom. He was giving a new sense of direction for this exodus. He spoke as though he knew that he was about to die and he saw it as part of the advent of this new Kingdom. The Last Supper was the launch pad for the Kingdom of God. Paul has added the command 'Do this in remembrance of me'.

It was a simple, straightforward command. 'Break bread and drink wine in remembrance of me.' I have obeyed that command for seventy-five years and I know that Jesus is really present in me.

All that I can add is that I have made my communion in every brand of Christian body … I have tried to clear my mind of dogma ... and obeyed the command. It works for me.

Sadly many Christians claim the 'right' of having the true faith … if you are not in communion with them, you are nothing. I wonder what Jesus would make of it. I am right and you are wrong makes a mockery of the cross.

To summarise, Jesus had taken the basic Passover concept of deliverance, and given us a covenant to follow …

this was the new return from exile. Above all, he saw himself as the person who would bring this to fruition. He was announcing the end of the present age and the birth of the new.

It had all come together at a point in history … the end of the temple, the new covenant at the Last Supper and the cruelty at Golgotha. All his life he had battled against evil. Now he had to face the ultimate decision. It was made at Gethsemane.

He had to face the wrath of Rome and be prepared to die for it. He had to face the evil stupidity of people who had no time for the poor and the sinners, the sick and the blind and the deaf … they mattered to Jesus. To defend their right for life Jesus now knew that he had to die if necessary. He had to prove that the God of Love would always prevail. He had to show that whatever happened in life, God would be there with you all the way. He did wobble at Gethsemane, but his trust in God stood firm to the end. That there is nothing that love cannot face is correct.

Bishop Wright in his wonderful book, 'Jesus and the Victory of God' says this: 'Jesus therefore took up his own cross. He had come to see it … not merely of Roman oppression … but the way of love and peace … it was the means of the victory of God.'

Jesus died for me.

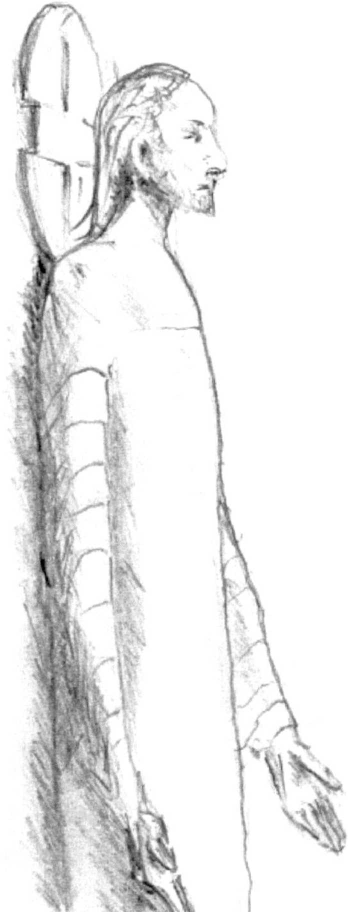

Chapter Ten

GOLGOTHA

Gethsemane was the final throw of the dice. I believe that Jesus could have walked away from it all. He had to make a decision. The agony was evident.

'After singing the Passover Hymn, they went out to the Mount of Olives. And Jesus said, "You will all fall from your faith; for it stands written: 'I will strike the shepherd down and the sheep will be scattered.' Nevertheless, after I am raised again I will go on before you into Galilee." Peter answered, "Everyone else may fall away, but I will not." Jesus said, "I tell you this: today, this very night, before the cock crows twice, you yourself will disown me three times." But he insisted and repeated: "Even if I must die with you, I will never disown you." And they all said the same.

When they reached a place called Gethsemane, he said to his disciples, "Sit here while I pray." And he took Peter and James and John with him. Horror and dismay came over him, and he said to them, "My heart is ready to break with grief; stop here, and stay awake." Then he went forward a little, threw himself on the ground, and prayed that, if it were possible, this hour might pass him by. "Abba, Father," he said, "all things are possible to thee; take this cup away from me. Yet not what I will, but what thou wilt."

He came back and found them asleep; and he said to Peter, "Asleep, Simon? Were you not able to keep awake for one hour? Stay awake, all of you; and pray that you may be spared the test; the spirit is willing, but the flesh is weak." Once more he went away and prayed. On his return he found them asleep again, for their eyes were heavy; and they did not know how to answer him. The third time he came and said to them, "Still sleeping? Still taking your ease? Enough! The hour has come. The Son of Man is betrayed to sinful men. Up, let us go forward! My betrayer is upon us." Suddenly, while he was still speaking, Judas, one of the Twelve, appeared, and with him was a crowd armed with swords and cudgels, sent by the chief priests, lawyers, and elders. Now the traitor had agreed with them upon a signal "The one I kiss is your man; seize him and get him safely away." When he reached the spot, he stepped forward at once and said to Jesus, "Rabbi", and kissed him. Then they seized him and held him fast. One of the party drew his sword, and struck at the High Priest's servant, cutting off his ear. Then Jesus spoke: "Do you take me for a bandit, that you have come out with swords and cudgels to arrest me? Day after day I was within your reach as I taught in the temple, and you did not lay hands on me. But let the scriptures be fulfilled." Then the disciples all deserted him and ran away. Among those following was a young man with nothing on but a linen cloth. They tried to seize him; but he slipped out of the linen cloth and ran away naked.'

Mark 14. 26-52.

That is a graphic account and smacks of reality. I believe that it was almost an eye witness account. It is probable that the young man who escaped naked leaving his cloak behind was Mark himself. The other Gospels do not mention the incident, which surely adds nothing to the account, except a personal touch. 'I was there! I saw it all'. It cannot be proved. It has been suggested that this Gospel was dictated to Mark by Peter and you can almost sense the tension as the tale was told yet again. Peter also makes it a personal testimony. All of this writing has the ring of truth.

The disciples must have realised that everything was changing. Jesus was different. The certainty had gone. He took Peter, James and John … the inner circle … with him and could not conceal his distress. He needed to pray.

As a child I was taught in Sunday School a little jingle which has never failed me.

'When I pray, I speak to God,
When I listen, God speaks to me.'

I wonder whether Jesus was taught much the same in his childhood synagogue in Nazareth. That is where he was taught and studied the Scriptures.

Jesus needed to pray. When he addressed God, he called him 'Abba'. That could be translated as 'Daddy'. And remember that Peter was there and he heard the word used. When the chips were down, it was a cry from the heart. "Daddy, Father, take this cup away from me! You can do that! But … not what I want, but what you want."

He knew what he had to do. "You can carry on sleeping now, it no longer matters … get up, let's go!" There were to be darker moments ahead for Jesus, far darker than we can begin to understand. Jesus was going to feel 'god-forsaken'. He was to feel deserted by his father. He had already told his disciples that they would abandon him and he now was to face the ultimate dereliction.

Every ounce of my being asks "Why? Why can anyone ask this of anyone? Where is love? How can a God of Love allow this betrayal?" As I write this, I am struggling to find the answer.

The story moved on to the high priest, the elders and the scribes and Peter followed at a distance. The question was asked.

'"Are you the Messiah, the Son of the Blessed One?"
Then the High Priest stood up in his place and questioned Jesus: "Have you no answer to the charges that these witnesses bring against you?" But he kept silence; he made no reply. Again the High Priest questioned him: "Are you the Messiah, the Son of the Blessed One?" Jesus said, "I am; and you will see the Son of Man seated on the right hand of God and coming with the clouds of heaven." Then the High Priest tore his robes and said, "Need we call further witnesses? You have heard the blasphemy. What is your opinion?" Their judgement was unanimous: that he was guilty and should be put to death.'
Mark 14. 63-65.

The real offence in the eyes of the accusers was his attack on the Temple and all that it stood for. Even the claim that he was the Messiah was in their terms all part of his delusions. As far as they were concerned there was no way in which he was the Messiah. It was laughable. But this was the man who talked about a Kingdom … that was different. If the Roman governor was informed that here was a rebel who was trying to set himself up as a king, there was only one outcome … crucifixion. The political game could be played.

But what about Peter? I believe that he was a brave man. The rest of the disciples had gone into hiding. They must have begun to wonder what it had all been about. The betrayal by Judas, the soldiers, the arrest, the accusations, it was all going to end in one way. The streets were now dangerous.

But Peter had other thoughts. Someone had to find out what was afoot. Of course it would be dangerous. I suspect that he pulled his cloak about him and ventured into the courtyard of the high priest's house. He actually heard the exchanges between the high priest and Jesus and remembered them well. He moved as close as possible and in the light of brazier he was recognised by a servant girl.

'Meanwhile Peter was still in the courtyard downstairs. One of the High Priest's serving-maids came by and saw him there warming himself. She looked into his face and said, "You were there too, with this man from Nazareth, this Jesus." But he denied it: "I know nothing," he said; "I do not understand what you mean." Then he went outside into the porch; and the maid saw him there again and began to say to the bystanders, "He is one of them"; and again he denied it. Again, a little later, the bystanders said to Peter, "Surely you are one of them. You

must be; you are a Galilean." At this he broke out into curses, and with an oath he said, "I do not know this man you speak of." Then the cock crew a second time; and Peter remembered how Jesus had said to him, "Before the cock crows twice you will disown me three times." And he burst into tears.'
Mark14. 67-71.
The game was up. He remembered the words of Jesus and it broke his heart. Of course he had denied all knowledge of Jesus. What else could he have done? He had hung around for as long as possible. It was time to leave.

So he went back to the other disciples to tell his story. It had been a fearful experience to see his master mocked and belittled and it was true, he had denied all knowledge of his Lord. Yet Jesus had prepared him for it and Peter was man enough to accept his failure, even though his intentions had been correct.

'When morning came the chief priests, having made their plan with the elders and lawyers and all the Council, put Jesus in chains; then they led him away and handed him over to Pilate. Pilate asked him, "Are you the king of the Jews?" He replied, "The words are yours." And the chief priests brought many charges against him. Pilate questioned him again: "Have you nothing to say in your defence? You see how many charges they are bringing against you." But, to Pilate's astonishment, Jesus made no further reply.

At the festival season the Governor used to release one prisoner at the people's request. As it happened, the man known as Barabbas was then in custody with the rebels who had

committed murders in the rising. When the crowd appeared asking for the usual favour, Pilate replied, "Do you wish me to release for you the king of the Jews?" For he knew it was out of spite that they had brought Jesus before him. But the chief priests incited the crowd to ask him to release Barabbas rather than Jesus. Pilate spoke to them again: "Then what shall I do with the man you call king of the Jews?" They shouted back, "Crucify him!" "Why, what harm has he done?" Pilate asked. They shouted all the louder, "Crucify him!" So Pilate, in his desire to satisfy the mob, released Barabbas to them; and he had Jesus flogged and handed him over to be crucified.'
Mark 15 1-15.

There were thousands of crosses in the Roman world and there were thousands more after the death of Jesus. You did not have to commit much of a crime to win a cross. There was no need for much of trial. It was more a sport than a legal transaction. One more crucifixion would not matter. The aim was to get the season of Passover done and dusted so that life could carry on. This crucifixion was not in the least important. Who cared!

The charge? Six times Mark spells it out … 'The King of the Jews'. This was pure politics, but not terribly important. Pilate did not even attempt to arrest any of the so-called followers of this criminal. They were not dangerous enough.

Pilate knew it was a futile accusation … there was no revolt. This man was not dangerous. It was all words. This man was innocent. There was a neat way to avoid the problem. Barabbas got Pilate off the hook. The crowd fell for it and

Pilate could wash his hands of the whole affair. It was not very important anyway.

Incidentally, there is a fable that Barabbas did turn up at Golgotha and with his hand on his heart said: "He died for me, I must live for him." That's good pulpit material, but in reality I suspect that he was sitting in a tavern in his cups celebrating with his right-wing mates. He had got away with it.

'Then the soldiers took him inside the courtyard (the Governor's headquarters) and called together the whole company. They dressed him in purple, and having plaited a crown of thorns, placed it on his head. Then they began to salute him with, "Hail, King of the Jews!" They beat him about the head with a cane and spat upon him, and then knelt and paid mock homage to him. When they had finished their mockery, they stripped him of the purple and dressed him in his own clothes.

Then they took him out to crucify him. A man called Simon, from Cyrene, the father of Alexander and Rufus, was passing by on his way in from the country, and they pressed him into service to carry his cross.

They brought him to the place called Golgotha, which means 'Place of a skull'. He was offered drugged wine, but he would not take it. Then they fastened him to the cross. They divided his clothes among them, casting lots to decide what each should have.

The hour of the crucifixion was nine in the morning, and the inscription giving the charge against him read, 'The king of the Jews.' Two bandits were crucified with him, one on his right and the other on his left.

The passers-by hurled abuse at him: "Aha!" they cried, wagging

their heads, "you would pull the temple down, would you, and build it in three days? Come down from the cross and save yourself!" So too the chief priests and the doctors of the law jested with one another: "He saved others," they said, "but he cannot save himself. Let the Messiah, the king of Israel, come down now from the cross. If we see that, we shall believe." Even those who were crucified with him taunted him.'
Mark 15. 16-32.

For the soldiers it was a bit of fun. If this man was a king, dress him up and let's have a laugh. It was no more than that. Yet another crucifixion … rather boring! So they were to get the dice out and idle the time away until they could get back to barracks.

Jesus was too weak to carry the cross beam on his shoulders and Simon gave a helping hand. We do not know why. Maybe he was a follower of Jesus. Mark states that he was the father of Alexander and Rufus … an odd piece of information unless it was relevant. We don't know, but in Romans 16. 13 Paul sends greetings to Rufus in the Roman Church. Rufus would have heard the tale from his father and I like to think that Rufus was alongside Peter in Rome together with Mark as they recorded the events. Mark could not resist this personal reference to Rufus's father. This was a second-hand witness account.

Golgotha was nicknamed the 'skull' because of its shape. It was the common place for crucifixions. The event of that day was almost too harrowing to write about. It was a fearful place.

'At midday darkness fell over the whole land, which lasted till three in the afternoon; and at three Jesus cried aloud, "Eli, Eli, lema sabachthan", which means, "My God, my God, why hast thou forsaken me?" Some of the passers-by, on hearing this, said, "Hark, he is calling Elijah." A man came running with a sponge, soaked in sour wine, on the end of a cane, and held it to his lips. "Let us see", he said, "if Elijah is coming to take him down." Then Jesus gave a loud cry and died. And the curtain of the temple was torn in two from top to bottom. And when the centurion who was standing opposite him saw how he died, he said, "Truly this man was a son of God."
Mark 15. 33-39.
Matthew adds the story of the earthquake. Luke adds the saying "Father into thy hands I commend my spirit"

"My God, my God, why hast thou forsaken me?" are heart-searching words, but should be placed in context. They are part of Psalm 22 and Jesus would have known it by heart. Jesus would have been recalling the psalm … he probably had learnt it during his youth. It starts with this cry of despair, but the psalm moves on to a firm acceptance … 'All the ends of the earth shall remember and turn to the Lord; and all the families of the nations shall worship before him.' All was well. God will never abandon you. It is not a psalm which ends with sadness, but with wonder and glory.

The other Gospels use the phrase that it was 'finished'. Again that has a far deeper meaning. The Greek word for finished has overtones. It means that what had to be done was 'utterly and completely finished, the task was done, it had truly been completed'. It was time for the last breath. The battle was over.

The symbolism of the torn veil of the Temple is lost on us, but not to the Jews. The veil concealed the inner sanctum, the Holy of Holies, where the high priest just once a year entered to plead with God on behalf of the nation. Mark more than suggests that the veil was no longer needed. The miracle had been achieved. God was no longer contained in the Temple. The Temple was no longer needed. God was now in every person's heart. That was what the battle had been about. God never leaves you. There is no veil. The work of Jesus had been completed … it was finished.

An innocent man had taken all the evil that man could do and, hand in hand with God, had seen it through to the end. Whatever this world throws at us, man cannot be destroyed.

On the cross Jesus suffered as a man and it was as a man that he achieved his victory. That victory was for us.

This is the crux of the crucifixion. There is nothing that man cannot face … his God is always with him. Whatever happens in your life, your God is right there alongside you. Jesus proved that to be true. Christ is our King.

Early Christians realised that Christ was King. That was the true Gospel. They had grasped the true meaning of the gospel. We are part of the Kingdom of God and Jesus is our King. He is our Majestas.

Incidentally, a Majestas had been placed on the outside west face of the twelfth century Cathedral in Llandaff and I am delighted that it is now, after all these centuries, safely inside

the building ... exceedingly tired and worn, but still a Majestas.

During my years of worship in the Cathedral, I faced the Epstein Majestas every morning at half six and every evening going about my daily prayer. The question was asked every time ... 'Is Christ your King?' It is a question not one of us can avoid. If your answer is negative, it is not too late. It is never too late, because God will never let you go and that is a guarantee. It was the message of Golgotha.

'He died for us and we must live for him' ... now!

This was not really understood at first in the early church. They thought that there would be a 'second coming', that Jesus would return. It is true that most texts infer that the second coming is not imminent, but the destruction of Jerusalem and Temple after the Jewish revolt, AD 66-70 encouraged the people to think that the 'end' was near and Jesus would come to their rescue. They were still hooked on the hope of a political kingdom. They did not understand that the Kingdom of God had arrived already.

'In fact, the Kingdom of God is among you.'
Luke 17. 20.

We rarely quote from the Gospel of Thomas. The question was … where is this Kingdom? The answer in the Gospel of Thomas was 'The Kingdom is within you and it is outside you'.

The Gospels reflect this thought. 'Search, and you will find; knock and the door will be opened.' Luke 11. 19. That is Kingdom talk. There is no need to amplify the thought with more examples.

God's will for us is simple. Open your eyes. Look around you. When Jesus said 'Follow me', he meant 'Do it now!' The Kingdom is here about you. You are part of this Kingdom.

Mark at the beginning of his Gospel spells out the purpose of Jesus … 'The time is fulfilled and the Kingdom of God is at hand'. It was not about heaven, but about earth. It was not a political kingdom, but the Kingdom of God. It is about the transformation of this world. This is the 'good news' and it is for all of us.

Jesus the man endured all that this world could fling at him and survived in a spectacular way. There was nothing that could deflect the love of God that is in man. In truth he died to prove that we can live in the Kingdom. His God never deserted him, but was with him every step of the way. The Kingdom of God is ours.

Perhaps it is time to explain the phrase … 'he survived in a spectacular way'! We call it the Resurrection.

The cross of the old Coventry Cathedral, made from the burnt wood of the destroyed roof

Chapter Eleven

THE GREATEST MIRACLE OF THEM ALL

Jesus was dead. He had been executed by the Roman soldiers by crucifixion, a death reserved for slaves and the basest of criminals. There was no honour in his death.

'taking the form of a slave...
And became obedient to the point of death –
Even death on a cross.'
Philippians 2.7-8.

And as far as the disciples were concerned, that was it. It was over. Jesus was dead. They had all failed him and gone into hiding. Peter had done his best, but even for him it was finished. All that was left was for a few women to bid farewell in their own way.

Jesus was dead. The normal Roman practice after a crucifixion was to leave the body hanging on the cross, to be picked at by the birds and animals. There were hundreds of such crosses on the Appian Way as one entered Rome. Human trash! They did not deserve burial. During the siege of Jerusalem in AD 69-70 there were thousands of Jews left to weather on their crosses. However, it was the Jewish custom to bury the body as soon as possible after death and the Roman authority understood that. They would have allowed the burial of Jesus.

Of course there was confusion and many theories

have been put forward through the ages to explain away the resurrection. Did those women look in the wrong tomb? Others think that he did not really die on the cross and that he recovered in the tomb and then returned to his startled disciples. There are, of course, conspiracy theories … it was a tale all cooked up by the disciples and, one assumes, with the agreement of Jesus himself.

However, it is safe to assume that Jesus was buried in the way that the Gospels have stated. Joseph of Arimathea was an important citizen of Jerusalem, and Pilate would have allowed him to arrange the burial. We can accept that Mary Magdelene and Mary, the mother of Joses, had checked where the grave was located.

'The women who had accompanied him from Galilee followed after; they took note of the tomb and observed how his body was laid. Then they went home and prepared spices and perfumes.'
Luke 23. 55.

That was late on that Friday afternoon. Then came the Sabbath. On the following morning, early, 'Mary Magdalene, and Mary the mother of James, and Salome, had brought sweet spices, that they might come and anoint him.'
Mark 16. 1.

We all know what happened next. The stone over the entry was rolled back. The absence of the body was too much for the mourners and the stage was set for the improbable to happen.

I once attended a lecture by the famous … or infamous to some … Bishop David Jenkins. He said: 'There are about thirty of us here and thus we have thirty ideas about the resurrection.' In other words, there can never be certainty. Can we all be right? Or are we all wrong?

That was a good question. You cannot suspend judgement on the resurrection of Jesus. It is central to all Christian belief and must be faced. To find an answer, we really have to examine the accounts and then come to a conclusion. 'Have faith and believe' is not acceptable as a statement. I need more than that. I am looking for certainty.

Incidentally, the empty tomb is not a proof of the resurrection. It is just an empty tomb. That is all that it is … an empty tomb. Another thought is that no-one considered a search for the body … if you question the resurrection that would have been the first thing to do.

Put Matthew, Mark, Luke and John alongside each other and you immediately have problems of conflicting evidence. My first reaction is that this is what you should expect, there can only be confusion and, if there were not, the stories would be totally suspect. That is the nature of stories and memory. At least it is obvious that something quite extraordinary had happened and we dare not ignore it. The punch line, the bottom line, is that something truly dramatic happened.

Perhaps the most startling fact is that after the death of Jesus, those disciples became followers and they made belief in the resurrection central to their faith. The eleven men were in hiding, totally disillusioned and disappointed. Within a matter of weeks they were preaching the resurrection. Peter said "God raised him from the dead, of that we are witnesses." If that was not true, anyone could have come forward and replied, "That's nonsense; I can show you the body." And all of this was within a mile or two from where the crucifixion had taken place. Take away the resurrection and you have little left. If there had not been the resurrection, Jesus would quickly have disappeared in history. It was the resurrection which transformed the disciples … eventually they were to die for their faith in Jesus.

Paul's first letter to the Corinthians, chapter fifteen, is still read at most modern day funerals. It is generally misunderstood. The Greek is translated into 'physical body' and 'spiritual body'. It sounds like a physical body and a ghostly body … two separate bodies. However, Paul's letter to the Romans 8. 9-11 rather contradicts this.

'If the Spirit of him who raised Jesus from the dead lives in you, he who raised Christ from the dead will give life to your mortal bodies also through his Spirit which dwells in you.'

That is very clear. There is no new body, but new life in your mortal body. Resurrection is the Spirit in your present body. This is my 'new' body in the Kingdom of God. My body remains the same, but the Spirit of Jesus is in me … now.

Is this what happened to Jesus? All four Gospels seem just to tell a story with no explanation. They are reporting what was seen. They are eyewitness accounts. In fact there appears to be very little editing. Jesus is a mundane human being … he walks, he talks, and he eats fish. His body has remained the same. There is no transfiguration, no flashing lights, no stardom.

The Gospels never suggest that we shall go to heaven when we die. They never say we shall be raised like Jesus.

What they really say is that he is raised and a new world has begun and we are part of it. In the end the disciples are told to go back to Jerusalem and await the Spirit of God. In fact they were at such a loss that they needed the Spirit of God to put life into them … they needed new life in their mortal bodies!

I believe that those disciples actually did meet a risen Lord and can think of no other plausible explanation. There are numerous implausible theories, but they all fall apart.

Who said 'If it walks like a duck, quacks like a duck and looks like a duck, it probably is a duck!

I find no way of disbelieving that Jesus was raised from the dead, leaving an empty tomb, and was briefly seen by normal human beings and their lives were transformed. The transfiguration was in them!

The tomb was empty, he was raised from the dead, and he did appear in a form that could be listened to and be touched.

Most certainly if there had not been this remarkable happening; we would now know nothing about him. He would have been just another Jew killed off by the Roman soldiery. He might have earned a line or two as others have in some distant unimportant document, but no more than that. The pre-Easter Jesus would have died in the dust of Golgotha and been long forgotten.

It would have been too easy at the time to prove that the tomb was not empty. The disciples had become a rabble. In fact what happened was open and really public knowledge. The women talked, they all talked and they were all puzzled. It really did not make much sense. The paparazzi would have had a field day. In fact it was all so puzzling that they could only talk about what had happened. There was no time to create a conspiracy theory.

And what did happen? Communicating any story is never easy … we all select our own words and tell it in our own way. Let's go off on a slight tangent.

Carl Burke was a Chaplain in Erie County Jail in New York. His problem was how to communicate with the often hostile or indifferent youths from New York's toughest area. The world of West Side Story with no music and no glamour! Instead of trying to force the scriptures on these hard-to-teach youngsters, he encouraged them to retell the Bible stories in their own hip language. The only rule of the game was that they were to keep to the basic meaning of the Bible stories. He produced a book in 1966 entitled 'God is for Real, Man'. My copy is tattered and tired by usage. It certainly is not Shakespeare and will probably offend many purists.

Touchin' Is Believin'
The Story of Doubting Thomas
Luke 24:36-48; John 20:19-31

After Jesus busted outa the grave
He met two of his gang on a road.
Man! Were they ever spooked and surprised.
They ran like crazy to the place where the other guys were.
And started to tell who they seen.

Before they could say much, bingo!
Jesus was there.
Came right through the door,
And they couldn't figure that out either.
He said, "Peace!"
Good thing to say 'cause they was plenty scared
Knees shakin' and teeth jumpin'.
They thought for sure, this is a ghost.
And who wouldn't?
So Jesus says,
"What buggin' you?
I ain't no ghost."
"See, I got hands
And feet just like you guys.
Go ahead, touch me and see.
You know seein' is believing
Well, they couldn't fight that; so they believed,
But, man, were they still surprised.
Just about then Jesus says,
"What cha got to eat? I'm hungry."
So they gave him some fish fry.
After supper Jesus told them about how he busted out of the grave
And why,
So that they could get rid of their sin and all
Of the bad things they did, and some did plenty

The main reason for quoting that remarkable piece of

writing is that I think that it contains a proof of the resurrection. Read it again and see if you can spot it.

The writer has captured the surprise and shock of the disciples … 'knees shakin' and teeth jumpin' is surely a fair description of their mental trauma. Bingo! There he was and came right through the door. It was a conversation stopper. There was only one thing that Jesus could possibly say at that juncture.

"Cool it!"

Perhaps that would have been a better remembrance than Luke's rendition.

"Peace be with you."

The reason that I am labouring the point is that it smacks of the truth. That is how it was.

As Luke said, they were 'startled and terrified'. He showed them the wounds just to help them understand. If you were making this story up, there is no way that you would have made up the next bit!

"What cha got to eat? I'm hungry. And they gave him some fish fry."

Luke adds 'and he took it and ate it.'

This is surely an eye-witness account. The basic problem was that those disciples had given up. It was over and done with. There had to be something really dramatic to shake the disciples into belief. We call it the resurrection. Nothing else would have done.

That helps me to understand. I accept the fact of the resurrection. I have no doubts at all. But the question that needs to be asked is what did it actually mean to those disciples and also to me.

Acts is interesting.

'This Jesus hath God raised up, whereof we are all witnesses.'
Acts 2. 32.
'This Jesus whom you crucified, God has made him both Lord and Messiah.'
Acts 2. 36.

That was the message. He is not dead. He is Lord. He is the Christ, the King, the Messiah. However for us to understand that message is not going to be easy. It is amazing that a bunch of cowards were transfigured (that word again) in such a way that they could proclaim such a message. Let's make it even clearer.

Jesus lives.

Jesus is Lord.

That is the message I have to understand.

Incidentally, another atom bomb was needed for Paul. His writings are the closest in time to the resurrection days. Here was a man who devoted his life to debunking the early followers of Jesus … that was his calling. 'Let's put a stop to this nonsense here and now' was the main purpose of Paul's life. But Paul was stopped in his tracks. Jesus appeared for him … nothing else would have worked. As a result he was a changed man … he was transfigured. His message now was "I have seen the Lord!" And this was a few years after the Easter appearances … the word that he uses is 'appearance'. It was no dream, no ghost, no vision … he met Jesus on the road to Damascus and he became the most important apostle of all.

Paul could write. His letter to the folk in Philippi contains an important passage. He actually tells them to think like Jesus. 'Let the same mind be in you that was in Christ Jesus'. Then he wrote what was probably an early Christian hymn. Wonderful words!

'Let your bearing towards one another arise out of your life in Christ Jesus. For the divine nature was his from the first; yet he did not think to snatch equality with God, but made himself nothing, assuming the nature of a slave. Bearing the human likeness, revealed in human shape, he humbled himself, and in obedience accepted even death … death on a cross. Therefore God raised him to the heights and bestowed on him the name above all names, that at the name of Jesus every knee should bow … in heaven, on earth, and in the depths … and every name confess, 'Jesus Christ is Lord', to the glory of God the Father.'

Philippians 2. 5-11.

'Jesus Christ is Lord' was the first Christian Creed and as far as I am concerned that is our basic belief. Jesus Christ is Lord. Later on in his letter to the Philippians, Paul describes his life before he met Jesus as mere garbage … a better translation is actually 'dung'! Paul concludes, 'All I care for is to know Christ.' I agree!

It immediately put Paul on a collision course with Rome. Imperial Rome put Caesar on the throne … Paul gave Jesus 'a name above every name.' Paul never mentions the empty tomb, because for him Jesus was alive and lived in him. That changed his life.

But let's go back again. The earliest story of the post-Easter Jesus is found in Mark 16. 1-8. only eight verses. Matthew has 20 verses; Luke has 53 verses, John 56 verses in two chapters.

Mark does not report on any appearances of Jesus and ends very abruptly … early in the second century another ending had been added to Mark. The probability is that there is a page missing from the basic Mark's Gospel. That is pure surmise. The fact that all accounts have different details is not a source of worry.

Matthew, 28. 18-20, spells out the purpose of it all … 'make disciples of all the nations, obey my commands and remember that I will be with you to the end of time.' That is obviously a post-Easter message attempting to give a meaning to the resurrection. In other words, you have a job of work to do. It is called 'the great commission'. Don't worry about the future, there are things to do.

Luke, 24. 13-35, describes a meeting with Jesus by two of his followers who were leaving Jerusalem on the way to the village called Emmaus. If you remember, it was getting late and they asked the stranger to stay in their home. He broke bread with them and suddenly they knew who it was. This is again post-Easter and explains that Jesus will be known to us when we break bread. This is firmly a reference to the Eucharistic worship which developed early in the Christian church.

John 20. 19-29 tells the story of 'doubting' Thomas.

Again it is a lovely post-Easter story with the classic post-Easter acclamation spoken by Thomas "My Lord and my God!" It seems unfair to call Thomas 'doubting' after those words. The punch line is obviously for all post-Easter followers 'Blessed are those who have not seen and yet have come to believe.' Don't worry if you have not seen the resurrection Jesus.

I feel a little sorry for Thomas. Imagine being stuck with the title of 'doubting Tom'. Thomas was the first disciple to get it right. 'Jesus Christ is Lord' … the first Christian creed.

If you think about these stories, they are truly teaching parables. I am not questioning the veracity of the stories in any way, but I am saying that they speak directly to me. Let's repeat a vital phrase.

'Blessed are those who have not seen and yet have come to believe!'

Those words are true today and they apply to the vast majority of Christians. You are not a second class Christian if you have not seen.

I believe that the risen Christ came for a purpose to bludgeon those early disciples into becoming followers. If he had not done that, there would be no Christian Church and everything would have been finished on Golgotha. Happily, we can still today experience the presence of the risen Christ. The resurrection Christ had done its work.

Is there such a thing as a resurrection body? I am not sure. The Jesus of the Gospels was certainly no ghostly apparition. He could be touched, seen, heard, fed … all in the same way as he was before he died on the cross. He actually went out of his way to prove that his body was the same as it had ever been. That was vital to convince them that it was really the Jesus that had walked through Galilee. He was the same person … the same person whose life was entirely wrapped up in God. In a short time he was to end these appearances and the talk then would be of the Spirit. That surely means that the Spirit of Jesus will be there for the disciples … the Spirit of Jesus firmly alive in them. There was no resurrection body … it had been the same Jesus.

John Masefield wrote a play called The Trial of Jesus. Procula, the wife of Pilate, had been much troubled in a dream. She listened to Lentulus, the centurion in charge at Golgotha, as he reported on the events of that afternoon. When he had finished, Procula pulled the centurion aside and asked "Please tell again how the prisoner died."

Then she paused and looked at the soldier.

"Do you think he's dead?

"No, lady. He's let loose into the world where neither Jew nor Greek can prevent his truth."

And that is it. This risen Christ is not confined in space or time. He can still enter locked rooms and come into our lives. He is really present in our lives. Paul in 1 Corinthians 15. 35-50 talks about his spiritual body but does not define it. It is inexplicable. Paul tries very hard to put it into words … and, dare I say it, fails. It is back to the word 'love' again, you can not define it or see it or touch it, but you know when it is there.

I can feel the presence of my mother in my life fifty years after her death. I can still hear her voice. If I have a question, because I knew her and loved her, I know the answer to my question. My wife died nine years ago, but in a real sense as far as I am concerned she is not dead. I cannot see her or touch her, but I believe that she is as alive in me as ever she was. As long as I live, she lives. That surely is life after death and it is born of love and will never die. Is that what was meant by the Spirit. The Spirit of God can never die. The Spirit of Jesus can never die. If I know and love Jesus, he comes firmly into my life.

That for me is what the resurrection was all about. Jesus has been let loose into the world and he is there for all of us. He is not dead.

I experience the living Jesus in my life today. There is no need to explain that … it is a fact. Christ is really present.

Seventy years ago I shared coffee with a missioner in a Kardhoma Coffee House in Cardiff. The war was over and I was back at University. Out of the blue he placed a Bible in the centre of the coffee table and said: "Can you put your hand on this Bible and state that Jesus is your Lord?"

This was my atom bomb. There was only one possible answer.

Jesus is my Lord.

Chapter Twelve

THIS MIRACLE IS FOR ME

It had required a miracle to convince those disciples that he was alive. Surely they must have discussed the question ... 'What happens now?' Luke gives us the answer and it is the beginning of a saga that stretches through time to each one of us today. It is quite a story.

'He showed himself to these men after his death, and gave ample proof that he was alive: over a period of forty days he appeared to them and taught about the Kingdom of God. While he was in their company, he told them not to leave Jerusalem. "You must wait."'
Acts 1. 3.

Now they had their orders and the next 'happening' was what we call the Ascension. For disbelievers this was to be more gobbledegook and miracle nonsense. In fact it was basic commonsense. The need for the appearances was over and they had to come to an end.

The trouble with the Ascension story is that it involves antique cosmology. Flat earth made sense two thousand years ago.

'When he said this, as they watched, he was lifted up, and a cloud removed him from their sight.'
Acts 1. 9.

And what is your theory? Did he take off like a sputnik? At first, he was two inches off the ground, then twelve inches and shot up into the cloud. Where is he now? Is he still going and has he reached the edges of the Milky Way? Or maybe after the lift off, the launch was called off and he 'sort-of-disappeared'. Bingo … he's gone! That really seems nonsense.

The Ascension was nothing to do with movement in space, although many folk think that is exactly what Christians believe. Those disciples must have been equally confused. It was like a game … now you see him, now you don't and now he seems to have gone altogether. They only had words to describe what was happening and they did their best. 'Heaven' and 'earth' to them had nothing to do with location; they were places where God was at work. God was everywhere and that was the only way that they could describe it. He was 'down here' and 'up there' and if he was not 'down here', he had to be 'up there'.

The Ascension had little to do with time. Try this. Luke had a neat arrangement in his writing. Easter – forty days – Ascension. Luke seems to be tidying up the events so that we can understand them. It was the start of the Christian calendar. Forty was a magic number. The Israelites when they escaped from Egypt were to spend forty years in the wilderness. Jesus after his baptism by John the Baptist spent forty days in the wilderness. Forty was the time that was needed to consider anything to do with God … at the end of that time God would act. So Luke has divided the events into time.

I repeat that the Ascension is really to do with Jesus and God and Jesus being 'let loose' into the whole world. He was released via heaven into the world.

'Do you think that he is dead?'

'No, lady, he's not dead, but let loose into the whole world!'

Christ is our King and rules over us. 'God has exalted him and given him a name which is above every name; that at the name of Jesus every knee should bow, of things in heaven, and things on earth, and things under the earth.'

The Ascension asserts the sovereignty of Jesus Christ. There is no part of my life that he cannot reach. Christ is King.

It is not a fairy story from a pre-space age. It is a simple statement that Jesus is Lord over all things and all people.

The order given to the disciples by Jesus was to stay in Jerusalem and wait.

'Then they returned to Jerusalem from the hill called Olivet, which is near Jerusalem, no further than a Sabbath day's journey. Entering the city they went to the room upstairs where they were lodging: Peter and John and James and Andrew, Philip and Thomas, Bartholomew and Matthew, James the son of Alphaeus and Simon the Zealot, and Judas the son of James. All these were constantly at prayer together, and with them a group of women, including Mary, the mother of Jesus, and his brothers.'

Acts 1. 12-14.

The whole gang was there, still puzzled and excited. What next?

'While the day of Pentecost was running its course they were all together in one place, when suddenly there came from the sky a noise like a strong driving wind, which filled the whole house where they were sitting … and they were all filled with the Holy Spirit.'
Acts 2. 1-4.

Yet another wow happening. Here we go again! Time for a story.

Some thirty-five years ago, I was in the bar at Kingston House … the headquarters of the Mersey Mission to Seamen in the heart of Liverpool … and I was clutching a 'Padre's Special'. Don't get excited, that was a half tankard of half an inch of Watney's Red Barrel topped up with lemonade … no wonder my teeth fell out! Alongside was a seafarer who had just come in from Portland on the east coast of America. I have no memory of how the subject emerged in our casual chat, but out of the blue I recall his question.

"What's all this talk about the Holy Spirit?"

That put me on the spot as I had to give an answer that he could understand. Happily I remembered what I had been taught in Sunday School as a child by a coal miner called Reg Hutchins.

"The Holy Spirit is the little bit of God inside me."

My seafaring companion was quiet for moment and then faced me with another poser.

"Are you telling me that all Christians have a little bit of God inside them?"

"Yes, I am. It's rather crude language, but I really believe that all Christians have a little bit of God inside them."

The pause was even longer and then he made a statement which I regard as one of the most perceptive statements that I have ever heard.

“In that case, if that is true, we should be able to see him!”

Wow!

When Paul wrote to the folk in Galatia he was saying the same thing. If you really have the Holy Spirit, it should show in your life. How can you judge that the Spirit of Jesus is in you? Paul simply said the harvest will be obvious to all.

‘The harvest of the Spirit is love, joy, peace, patience, kindness, goodness, fidelity, gentleness and self-control.’

Galatians 5. 22-23.

If Jesus taught us anything, I’ll settle for that lot.

In fact I believe that most of us have all those qualities, but there is still a problem … it’s almost impossible to have them all at the same time. But please note the first gift of the Spirit is love. Read that list again and I am certain that you will agree that, as an agenda for those who would be in the Kingdom of God, the list is perfect.

Cranmer and his Book of Common Prayer have much to answer for. He endlessly uses the phrase Holy Ghost. It troubled me as child as I imagined God arriving in a white bed-sheet and making banshee noises.

Remember that young convict in New York and his remarkable prose?

‘Came right through the door,

And they couldn’t figure that out either.

“I ain’t no ghost.

See, I got hands
And feet just like you guys,
Go ahead, touch me and see."

Eventually, as I grew up, the word 'ghost' was dropped in churches and 'spirit' replaced it. Incidentally I still meet pious folk who think that we have debased the language as they are convinced that Jesus spoke in a seventeenth century lingo.

The trouble is that all we have are words. If you want a problem, tackle the Holy Trinity … God is Father, Son and Holy Ghost. Incidentally, if I had some difficulty with the word 'ghost', many years back a young man said to me, "If God's like my father, forget it!"

The idea of the Holy Trinity emerged quite early in the Christian church and has produced its own problems of misunderstanding. I recall once I was part of a quiz panel and the question was 'Can you explain the Holy Trinity?' I think I said that an explanation would not help you in any way to understand God. That went down with an audience groan and a bright-eyed young teacher sounded off about the three-leaved clover being one plant. Perhaps I should have said look at your mother … one person, but a wife, a mother and a grandmother … one person. Most Vicars with any sense ask the Curate to preach on Trinity Sunday.

College did not help me. I never could make sense of the Athanasian Creed's remarkable language … 'The Father incomprehensible, the Son incomprehensible, the Holy Ghost incomprehensible' … and so it was. We used to recite that Creed with the congregation on all feast and high days. How has the Christian faith arrived at such gobbledegook? Dogma has become airborne and taken us with it. Of course I can discuss how this makes theological sense and even mention Thomas Aquinas in passing, but what happened to that first Christian Creed … 'I believe that Jesus Christ is Lord'? We seem to have travelled a long way from the start of it all.

Back to basics is a common phrase these days. Let's do it. Back a bit. In the Old Testament in Leviticus 19. 18 we read: 'Thou shalt love thy neighbour as thyself.'

And it occurs again and again … Mark 12. 31; Matthew 19. 19; Luke 10. 27; and Romans 13. 9; Galatians 5. 14; James 2. 8 and on and on.

This word 'love' seems to be a rather basic concept. If I were placed on a desert island and only allowed one chapter of the Bible, there would be no problem of the choice. Take 1 Corinthians 13. It says it all for me.

'I may speak in the tongues of men or angels, but if I am without love, I am a sounding gong or a clanging cymbal. I may have the gift of prophecy, and know every hidden truth; I may have faith strong enough to move mountains; but if I have no love, I am nothing. I may dole out all I possess, or even give my body to be burnt, but if I have no love, I am none the better.

Love is patient, love is kind and envies no-one. Love is never boastful, nor conceited, nor rude; never selfish, not quick to take offence. Love keeps no score of wrongs; does not gloat over other men's sins, but delights in the truth. There is nothing love cannot face; there is no limit to its faith, its hope, and its endurance.

Love will never come to an end. Are there prophets? Their work will be over. Are there tongues of ecstasy? They will cease. Is there knowledge? It will vanish away; for our knowledge and our prophecy alike are partial, and the partial vanishes when wholeness comes. When I was a child, my speech, my outlook, and my thoughts were all childish. When I grew up, I had finished with childish things. Now we see only puzzling reflections in a mirror, but then we shall see face to face. My knowledge now is partial; then it will be whole, like God's knowledge of me. In a word, there are three things that last for ever: faith, hope, and love; but the greatest of them all is love.'

I suggest that this is the most vital passage in the whole of scripture and, in fact, the theme is present in many of the great religions of the world. The conviction of the importance of this passage came very early in my life and that truly was a blessing because it has taken my eighty-six years to work out the full implication of the thoughts ... and I am still at it.

The study of this chapter has over time enabled me to live happily with most of the ecclesiastical baggage which I have acquired. I cannot stress the importance of carrying that baggage because in it there will be ultimate truth. In other words, keep the baggage, but get your feet on the ground. Freely I acknowledge that without the Church, the early hours of prayer on cold winter mornings, the pain of sharing the suffering of people and the barren periods of my pilgrimage through life, there would not have been a vehicle which could have carried me across the eight decades and, to change the metaphor, that very Church has proved to be the sounding board to test what has, at last, become the ultimate thought. That thought is so simple that I hesitate to voice it ... if there is no love, there is nothing. And the prime source as I have journeyed to uncover that apparently simple truth has always been 1 Corinthians 13.

Paul is the ideal person to give us help, not only because he has left us a vast amount of writing on matters spiritual, which have withstood some two thousand years without being discredited, but Paul has had the advantage of basing his writings on the contact he enjoyed with those who had personal contact with Jesus. Whilst we cannot uncover the 'ipsissima verba', the very words of Jesus, Paul does reflect their influence. If you feel the need to go 'back to basics', Paul is as good as any person to take you there.

'Without love, you are nothing.'

This chapter in Corinthians is the very soul and centre of religion, regardless of which religion that might be … the enduring power of love. You can judge all the world's religions by these guide-lines … that's another book! Corinthians spells religion out in language we can all understand and recognise. Don't fall into the trap of thinking that it is too simple, because it requires a lifetime to fathom its depths.

Religions of all kinds and sorts carry far too much baggage, collected over the centuries and this circumference of religion is too often confused for its centre. The baggage has produced almost unbelievable, unwise and subhuman controversy. The soul, the centre, of religion is love. That really should be framed, underlined and totally digested.

Let's look again at this word, which is the heart of

all true religion. Love is not just passion. Often there is no tenderness to be found in passion. Love is not just good nature ... and yet that is part of it. Love is not natural kindness. That can so often disappear at a whim. Am I saying that love is unnatural? Let's look at that thought.

It is easier for the strong to care (I've used a lesser word than 'love' just to make these points) for the weak. That can almost be natural. But, it is harder for the weak to care (or even love!) for the strong and is almost asking too much.

It is easier for the rich to care for the poor than for the poor to care for the rich.

It is easier for the beautiful to care for the ugly, but possibly tougher for the ugly to care for the beautiful.

We could continue these examples, but let's move along. When we are exhorted to 'love God' the relationship that we have with God is that of us being weak, poor and ugly, and thus we should not be surprised that it is difficult. Put simply, loving God is not a natural activity of man. How can it be? Of course the truth is that the concept of 'God' is truly beyond us, or at least beyond me.

I can only cope with the idea that I can find God in the image of Jesus. That is an important statement. The simple word 'God' has little meaning for me although I am fairly steeped in the intricate thoughts of theology and have spent a lifetime in the search. We have Jesus and as I have stated I can find and understand the meaning of love by meditating (that's only a posh word for 'thinking') about the life of Jesus. The Jesus figure makes all my understanding of God possible and, almost as a by-product, the meaning of that word love.

Greek was the superb language of the time and remains to this day unrivalled in expressing shades of meaning. So we must examine the Greek word for love. Paul uses *agape* and I'll return to it.

There are other Greek words for love.

eros (erotic, etc). This is, of course, physical love between man and woman. It does not appear in the New Testament.

storge. This is to do with family affection or love for one's nation.

philia (philosophy, love of knowledge, etc). This is the commonest word in the New Testament for love. It is a great word, friendship, the love of a husband and wife. The best translation is 'cherish' which is used in the 1662 Book of Common Prayer as part of the marriage vows. It expresses warmth.

In the Corinthians' chapter the word in Greek is *agape* and is an odd choice at first glance. The word is used in variant forms 250 times in the Bible and the problem is 'Why abandon the other Greek words for love?' The other words were probably regarded as unsuitable. *eros* had certainly been debased by usage with overtones of passion. *storge* was too narrowly associated with family. *philia* was restricted to the near and dear, a lovely word but not wide enough. So that leaves *agape,* a word rarely used in Classical Greek, but adopted in a big way by Paul.

Christian love (*agape)* must certainly extend to the nearest and dearest, but does go further, to friends, to the neighbour, to the enemy, to the entire world, and to fellow Christians. In other words, *agape* has to do with the mind … and not the heart. It is not an emotion which comes over us; it is a principle by which we deliberately live. No-one naturally loves an enemy. To do that you must conquer your emotions and natural inclinations. This is the power which enables us to love the unlovable, to love the strong, the rich, and the beautiful. It is an attitude of mind.

So what is the meaning of *agape*? The supreme passage is Matthew 5. 43-48.

'You have learned that they were told, "Love your neighbour, hate your enemy." But what I tell you is this: Love your enemies, and pray for your persecutors; only so can you be children of your heavenly Father, who makes his sun rise on good and bad alike, and sends rain on the honest and dishonest. If you love only those who love you, what reward can you expect? Surely the taxgatherers do as much as that. And if you greet only your brothers, what is extraordinary about that? Even the heathen do as much. You must therefore be all goodness, just as your heavenly Father is all good.'

We are told to love our enemies. Why? And get this answer! In order that we should be sons of God. The explanation goes on. God sends his rain on the just and the unjust and on the evil and on the good. This states so clearly that no matter what a man is like, God seeks nothing but his highest good. That is *agape.*

No wonder Paul starts the next chapter with a simple command. 'Put love first.'

There is no way that I can grasp this *agape* stuff on my own. I need help. That help is available to us all. The help available to us is, of course, the Spirit of God ... the Spirit of Jesus.

I am reminded of Padre Makin who served as Chaplain in Cardiff prison and then became the Vicar in the wilderness of Adamstown, alongside my patch in Tremorfa. During the war he had been a Chaplain in the Eighth Army in North Africa; he was a 'desert rat'. That really is what I call training in the ministry. We became good companions and this is one of his memories.

"The day had been hard and sunset was about to fall in a matter of minutes. I needed a quiet time and wandered away from our tanks, deep in thought. Suddenly I came to my senses; I had walked into a mine field. No-one could help me and I froze in my tracks. Help! Then I looked behind me and in the quickly fading light, I saw my footsteps in the sand … they had been safe. Gently I turned and put my feet surely into the prints. I was safe and had a sermon to be used many times after that."

Following the steps of our Lord is pure sermon material … for me it really does make sense. 'Lord, where do I put my footsteps next?' is a valid prayer and if you have grown to know him over the years of your life, you will know the answer.

That, I suspect, was how the church began. 'Lord, what now?' The answer was 'Walk in my footsteps.' Is that too simple? If you know me and love me, you will know what to do.

But those disciples needed help in a big way and it was given. However, before we talk about the miracle of the coming of the Holy Spirit, let's take this spirit-talk a pace at a time.

My dear old mother has long gone and probably is only remembered by me now. I can still hear her voice … and I mean hear … 'Robert!' Whenever I heard those strident tones, I knew that I was guilty as charged. Whenever all was well, I was addressed as Bob. But it goes further than that. In a real sense I can converse with her today sixty years later. Of course, I cannot touch her or see her, but I know what she would have me do. In other words, she is as alive for me today as ever. It is a helpful form of life after death.

My dear wife died ten years back. I had sat behind her at school at the age of eight. We knew each other! For me she is not dead, but alive. If there is life after death, this is it! As long as I live, she will never die. That is what love can do for you. There is no need for her to come through doors for me to touch her. Her spirit is fully alive in me. Her body was tired and worn out and could not continue. Her spirit is vibrant. Explain it as you may, we still walk hand in hand because love never dies. Again, I feel that this is life after death.

Is that what we mean when we talk about the Spirit of God? I have Jesus alive in me today. If my only knowledge of God's activity is in what I know about Jesus, it is enough for me. Surely this is the Resurrection. Jesus is alive in me today. The Resurrection is about today.

Bishop Tom Wright of Durham wrote this:

'Indeed, precisely because part of that new possibility is

for human beings themselves to be revived and renewed, the resurrection of Jesus does not leave us passive, helpless spectators. We find ourselves lifted up, set on our feet, given new breath in our lungs, and commissioned to go and make new creation happen in the world.'

That is the nub of the matter. It was as though Jesus at last got those disciples by the scruff of the neck, shook them and told them to get on with it. It was time for action. And that they did.

I seem to recall that I have read much about the Greek word *pneuma*, which is the word 'spirit'. Incidentally, we all use that Greek word almost daily … pneumatic tyres … we pump air into the tubes otherwise they are flat! This is the new breath and it is the breath of Jesus. No wonder they talked about the coming of the spirit like a wind sweeping them off their feet … 'a strong driving wind, which filled the whole house where they were sitting.' How else could they describe it?

I believe that the resurrection of Jesus and the spirit of Jesus is a today-happening giving life to me today. This enables me to walk in his footsteps. This is love in action and that is another story.